COOKING UP A STORM

The Misra Family Way

Suneeta & Susmita

First published in India in 2015 by:
Suneeta Mishra and Susmita Misra
misrafamilycookingupastorm@gmail.com

Copyright © 2015 Suneeta Mishra and Susmita Misra
Print Book ISBN: 9789384439248

Suneeta Mishra and Susmita Misra assert the moral right to be identified as the author of this work.

9789384439316 - Paperback
9789384439323 - Hardback

Publishing facilitation: AuthorsUpFront

All rights reserved. No part of this publication may be reproduced, stored in a retrieval system, or transmitted, in any form or by any means, without the prior written permission of the AUTHOR, or as expressly permitted by law, or under terms agreed with the appropriate reprographic rights organisations. Enquiries concerning reproduction outside the scope of the above should be sent to the AUTHOR.

Design & Graphic

Anjali Kumari
anjaliashish78@gmail.com

Photo Courtesy:

Suneeta Mishra (Atlanta)
Avirup Ganguly (Delhi NCR)

For Papa

MESSAGE

Dear Linoo and Lizoo

Reading and food have been the focus of the Misra family. So they are well read and well fed. With this cookbook, you two are managing to combine both these passions beautifully.

Parents feel an immense sense of pride when their children outshine them in any sphere; I am very happy that you have mastered the culinary art and love to entertain people with home cooked food. Whenever I have visited either of you, I have sampled some new and varied fare, innovative in terms of taste as well as presentation. Hope you will keep that up.

Your cookbook consists of Indian and global recipes; dishes that you have enjoyed over the years. Through the making of this book I was overwhelmed by how much you girls remember of those childhood meals. Since the recipes have been meticulously presented in easy steps and with detailed instructions, I am sure even beginners can cook these with confidence.

All the best.

With lots of love and blessings
Mama

Swarna Misra
Bhubaneswar

PROLOGUE

As one of the more prolific guinea pigs on the authors' culinary learning curve, it is but apt that I write a prologue to this fascinating collection of recipes (by means of introduction I am the youngest sibling of the co-authors). We grew up on a legend that our great-grandfather used to cook at weddings, even as he held a senior government day job with fancy titles et al. The tradition of men of the house intermittently dishing out tasty meals continued down two more generations, with yours truly being the proverbial black sheep. Perhaps, this work is also meant to be a reference point, as and when I decide to follow tradition.

While several cooks around never really spoilt the broth, one grew up in an environment where disproportionate time was devoted to food-researching, preparing and endless discussions around the meal that went by and the one immediately up ahead. Subsequent additions to the family, inherited gastronomic genes and that in turn spurred an enhanced level of interest and experimentation around the kitchen.

The authors are as different as chalk and cheese. One, an artist with an added flair for presentation. The other, methodical with the temperament of a research scholar. The former is a natural with singular focus on overwhelming each of the sensory faculties with food. The latter is a late bloomer with an equal, if obsessive eye on the health quotient.

This diverse collection of recipes brings together a potpourri of cuisines. It is also written in a lucid style that will prove useful to novices and experts alike. It brings together legacy family recipes, impromptu improvisations that were subsequently templated (and often nicknamed) and some others that were noted down when one came across innovative preparations. It is impressive how scores of hand written cookbooks (and loose sheets of paper) survived decades since compilation, several relocations and the odd natural disaster to find shape in this delightful cookbook. Hoping readers will embark on an exciting culinary journey of their own, thanks to this book.

Mahesh Misra
New Delhi

ACKNOWLEDGEMENTS

To start with we would like to thank our mother Swarna Misra from whom we learned the culinary basics. Right from when we were kids, we would see her continually experiment with different cuisines including having one of her recipes published in "Femina". Mama as we call her, encouraged us to publish and without her this book would have remained a distant dream.

Three people who would have been very pleased with this effort of ours are no longer with us. They deserve a mention for very different reasons. Our Grandfather Dr Sitikantha Misra who was a physician by profession, in spite of belonging to a generation which believed that men had no place in the kitchen, was a pretty darn good cook himself. And he regaled us with stories of his culinary adventures during his army days where he travelled abroad extensively and developed a palate for various kinds of foods, even the ones traditionally forbidden for Indians like – the steak! Our Grandmother Sarojini Misra or "Bou" as all of her kids and we grandkids called her was the actual chef of the family. Meticulous in her prep work and cooking down to the last garnish, she helped in schooling our discerning palates so to speak. Our father Dilip Misra was the real foodie in the family. It was fascinating how someone could love traditional cuisines and completely out of the box experimentative cooking with equal fervour. A great cook himself, his ideal day would be one in which he had south Indian breakfast, Chinese lunch and continental dinner.

Brother, Mahesh, who by his own admission has struggled through sampling our cooking from a very early age (and miraculously survived), does deserve a special mention. The fact that he now does indeed compliment our cooking speaks volumes on how far we have come. Sister in law Rinku who thankfully is a good cook and a foodie herself blended right in and provided constant encouragement and support by helping dig out lost recipes, giving her tips around plating, photographs and also lending her crockery for the pictures.

Both sets of in laws also indulgently put up with our cooking without any fuss and appreciating small wins. Mothers in laws also passed down their family recipes that we now cook and enjoy.

We are thankful to have a wide network of supportive friends who have helped in making this book a reality. Suneeta Patnaik shared with us her own publishing journey and gave us leads about publishers and followed up to check on us. Ankana Bhalla was very creative when it came to brainstorming names for the book title and ultimately the one all of us liked and went with "cooking up a storm" was hers. She also helped with the proofing. Jayanti Chowdhary spent hours on the book- proofing, giving us design ideas and most importantly connecting us with our graphic designer Anjali Kumari whose brilliant designs and concept ideas for the pages brought our vision to life. At Camp Delhi, Susmita's kitchen assistant Gita helped tirelessly to ensure that the cooking for the recipe pictures was flawless and seemed the most excited about the whole process. At Camp Atlanta, Shobha Swamy kept up Suneeta's waning enthusiasm at times and also lent her beautiful crockery for some of the photo shoots. And the numerous other friends who opened their kitchen and hearts to us; hope you find yourself in the stories.

Avirup Ganguly at Delhi took some amazing photographs and made the food look drool worthy.

Our husbands Unmesh Mishra and Sabyasachi Dasmohapatra deserve a special thanks for enduring our culinary experiments for years now, surviving, encouraging, appreciating and loving us in spite of it all.
Last but not the least, this book is for our children – Srishti, Kanishka, Sonakshi and Sankalp. The spark in your faces and smiles when mommy cooked something that you liked, made us feel like master chefs and was our ultimate reward. The polite "it's nice" accompanied with the food left on your plates, made us want to cook it better and more tailored to your tastes the next time. This book is for you and the future generations of Misra, Mishra and Dasmohapatras ... Hope someday you too will cook up a storm in your kitchens. With that thought ...bon apetit and happy cooking.

Suneeta Mishra

Suneeta Mishra was born in Bhubaneswar, India. A learning & development and HR professional, she worked in Kolkata for 10 years before moving to the United States in 2000. She presently works for a fortune 500 company in the area of corporate learning and development.

Growing up in a port town where dining on a ship from an entirely different part of the world was quite common, she was exposed to international cuisines from an early age. One of the perks of being raised in a small community where everyone knew everyone else, and came from different parts of India was developing an appetite for a very diverse food palate. She still remembers the wonderfully varied regional fare that her neighbours cooked and shared with everyone during festivals. A self-proclaimed foodie, she attributes her interest in cooking to her parents and grandparents who not only were great cooks, but also treated every meal as an elaborate family ritual, savouring every morsel and discussing the food long after the meal was over! Suneeta believes that simple, flavourful and good quality ingredients can take a dish from the bland to exceptional. According to her, magic in the kitchen begins when the cook is completely engaged and gives his/ her heart and soul to the cooking process. A maverick cook of sorts, Suneeta loves to indulge in fusion cooking, experimenting and combining uncommon ingredients to create her versions of traditional staples. Plating food in an artistic way to enhance its appeal and make the dish look good before it is put on the table is also important to her, as she believes that one feasts with one's eyes first.

Suneeta currently resides in Atlanta, Georgia with her husband Unmesh and daughters Srishti and Sonakshi. She enjoys travelling, food photography and volunteering at various charities in the greater Atlanta area. An avid blogger, she hopes to publish her first fictional novel soon. You can follow her food blogs at diehardfoodies.blogspot.com

Susmita Misra

Susmita grew up in Paradip, a port town along the East Coast of India. Being a "Customer and Shopper" Insights' specialist, and a nomad in her own right, she has lived and worked across India. Her work has taken her from Mumbai to Kolkata to Chennai to Delhi, spanning a vast expanse of over 10,000 miles and exposing her to several diverse cuisines. This gave her the opportunity to sample authentic regional delicacies and inspired her to infuse some of this into her own style of cooking. An avid traveller, she has also developed a keen International palate and always manages to take time out for good food wherever she maybe; capturing these flavours in her little kitchen too.

Her culinary journey though, started rather disastrously with burnt eggs and instant noodle dinners (albeit dinners her husband stomached irrespective). However years of learning and experimenting have now led her to innovate. She comes from a family of great cooks and the foodie genes have seemed to persist through generations. This is what she credits her edge to, when it comes to flavour or taste. Susmita claims that her food is a product of her passion meeting perseverance and rigor. And manages to add at least one new recipe to her repertoire each week in spite of a hectic work schedule. She champions home cooked food and is constantly encouraging her younger friends to start cooking and enjoying meals at home. Wholesome, low oil, no fuss, one pot recipes are her all-time favourites.

She currently lives in Gurgaon (India) with her husband Sabyasachi and sons, Kanishka and Sankalp. Her family serve as her food critiques with every recipe having to pass their muster, as well as her cheer leaders celebrating every new successful recipe. Susmita is a yoga practioner, blogger, enjoys travelling and ticking places off her bucket list. Some day she hopes to start a home dining service and professionally take to cooking. You can follow her food blog at yumeats.blogspot.in

INTRODUCTION

Food is priority for the Misra household sounds like an understatement; it is the sole focus. We live, breathe and dream about food. All our discussions lead to food and every meal, however simple, an elaborate ritual.

Growing up in a household where a wide variety of dishes were cooked, some more from the neighborhood sampled there was never a dull moment. While our grandmother stuck to traditional cooking and long handed down family recipes, our mother was constantly experimenting with different flavors and trying out new dishes. As a result we developed a very varied palate and were quite adventurous in trying out different recipes ourselves. When we got married, it was our turn to tinker around the kitchen. We cooked to impress in laws, we cooked to wow friends, we cooked to make fussy kids eat, we cooked to replicate traditional family favorites and sometimes, we cooked just for ourselves – for the culinary high that a chef gets when a dish is well done and tastes delicious.

This book is a journal of our culinary journey. It has an eclectic collection of recipes which have been neatly ordered into various categories for easy reading. They are recipes that we learnt from our Mom, in laws, other family members and friends and sometimes simply the result of experimenting with tried and tested recipes and adding ingredients to add our spin on it. We sisters are now older, have families of our own with very different palates, and live continents away from each other, food continues to be a bonding factor. It is quite normal for us to wake each other up at unearthly hours to discuss the menus for an upcoming dinner party and brainstorm ideas about which dessert will complement the food. What is also unique about this cookbook is the write up that precedes the recipes. They range from funny to informative to poignant and nostalgic, and offer you a slice of our personal stories and memories associated with the dishes. We hope you will enjoy going through this cookbook and enjoy cooking the Misra family way.

We would also love to hear back from you. Please send in your comments to misrafamilycookingupastorm@gmail.com

SOUPS, SALAD & BEVERAGES

Thai chicken coconut soup	18-19
Chicken tortilla soup	20
French onion soup	21
Pudina sherbet	22
Lemon ginger cooler	23
Tomato saar	24-25
Mango lassi	26-27
Watermelon cooler	28-29
Chicken larb	30
Carrot and raisin salad	31
Khamang kakdi	32-33
Mango kale sprout salad	34-35
Pinacorn salad	36-37

SNACKS & STARTERS

Dahibara aludam ghuguni	40-41
Fish cutlets	42-43
Quino upma	44-45
Sesame potatoes	46-47
Pao bhaji	48-49
Paneer kebabs	50
Baked gold coin prawns	51
Salami olive rolls	52-53
Hummus	54-55
Feta and watermelon sticks	56
Chutney sandwich with tadka	57
Baked cheesy onion dip	58
Hung curd dips	59

VEGETABLES & DAAL

Mocha ganto	62-63
Dalma	64-65
Avial	66
Kasa tarkari	67-68
Daal makhni	69-70
Buta dali with kakharu	71
Baked cabbage manchurian	72-73
Tandoori gobhi	74
Santula	75
Stuffed parwal	76-77

FISH, CHICKEN & MUTTON

Bhanga besara	80-81
Fish In banana leaves	82
Baked fish in white sauce	83
Prawn sweet and sour	84-85
Sorisa macha	86
Dahi macha	87
Macha haldi pani	88-89
Allepey fish curry	90
Prawn curry	91
Daab chingri	92-93
Ghee roast chicken	94-95
Chicken khus khus	96
Mexican chicken	97
Butter chicken	98-99
Khow suey	100
Chilli chicken	101
Chicken stew	102-103
Dhania chicken	104
Chicken shami kebab	105
Murgh kali mirch	106
Mutton vindaloo	107
Meat loaf	108-109
Spaghetti with meat balls	110-111
Moussaka	112
Saag gosht	113
Mutton curry rogan josh	114
Railway mutton curry	115

RICE, PILAF & CHUTNEYS

Lemon rice	118-119
Chicken pulao	120
Tiranga pulao	121
Curd rice	122-123
Corn methi pulao	124
Chinese konji	125
Chow chow	126-127
Basil rice	128
Kanika	129
Tomato and aam papad chutney	132
Green papaya raita	133
Dahi baigan	134-135
Peanut chutney	136
Guacomole	137

DESSERTS

Chocobanana cake	140-141
Apple and date cake	142-143
Caramel pudding	144-145
Lemon poppy seed cake	146-147
Thai black rice pudding	148-149
Bhapa doi	150-151
Gulab jamun	152
Rossogolla	153
Kaju barfi	154-155
Natural ice cream	156
Chena poda	157
Poda pitha	158
Low fat "Tiramisu"	159
Khus khus halwa	160-161
Monda pitha	162
Manga mousse pie	163

SALAD SOUP & BEVERAGES

THAI CHICKEN COCONUT SOUP
A delicately flavoured soup with coconut milk and chicken broth

In our family, we love everything Thai. When we moved to the US we were shocked at the quality of food at the Chinese buffets that are found in small little malls lining the highways. Invariably, the food there was greasy, deep fried, heavily sugared dishes that got passed around as Chinese food. It was astonishing to taste so much sugar in the dishes. So much so, that some of the chicken dishes could legally qualify as desserts! If you don't believe what I am saying, I dare you to try and eat in one of these buffets. I am sure no Chinese worth his salt ever ate there, although by George! they do seem to own all of them and thrive! On long drives, crossing a couple of states with kids who were toddlers then, these places were our quick bite go to places, when we were tired of the American fast food joints that typically dot the interstates. That's when we looked around for what we call as the Indian Chinese and ......discovered Thai! Unlike their Chinese counterparts, Thai food was usually more delicately flavoured, tangy and spicy and rarely that sweet. And typically, we would start our meals with 'Tom Kha Gai' which is a flavourful soup made with coconut milk and chicken broth. We just love this soup and many a times we go to a Thai restaurant just to have this soup. I started experimenting with some of the ingredients and arrived at this version of the soup which I think, comes really close to the original.

Ingredients

40 mins   **8 ppl**

Chicken broth: 6 cups

Ginger: 6 inch root cut into thin slices

Coconut milk: 1 ½ cups

Fish Sauce: 1 tbsp

Lemon zest: 1 tbsp

Lime juice: ¼ cup (Juice from about 3 limes)

Dhania(Coriander) leaves for garnish: 10 tender stems

Chicken: 1pound (boneless skinless chicken thighs cut into 1 inch pieces)

Mushrooms: Shitake or Oyster stemmed and caps cut into bite size slices

Sugar: 1tsp (Optional)

Salt: 1tsp (to taste)

Chilli (Red pepper) flakes: 1 tsp

Method

1. In a wok or a deep vessel, add ginger and lemon zest to the chicken broth and bring to a boil.
2. Strain and discard the ginger and zest.
3. Bring back to heat, adding the chicken and mushrooms and bring it to a boil.
4. Reduce heat and simmer, stirring occasionally, till the chicken is cooked through and mushrooms are soft. (About 20 minutes).
5. Add sugar, salt coconut milk and lemon juice. Stir once and remove from heat.
6. Pour into soup bowls, garnish with chilli flakes and coriander leaves.
7. Serve immediately.

Note:
For a vegetarian version of this dish, replace chicken broth with vegetable broth, add medium soft tofu cubes instead of chicken and skip the fish sauce entirely, adding a little flavoured vinegar in the end or chilli oil if needed.

CHICKEN TORTILLA SOUP
My take on a Mexican favourite

Having a varied palate and a child who loves Mexican and Spanish food, we do tend to frequent restaurants that serve Mexican food. Tortilla soup is what I always ask for, when I visit these restaurants. To my utter surprise, the recipes differ vastly in every restaurant. My absolute favourite is the one they serve in a small little place called Soho in Atlanta. Soho serves very eclectic food and their tortilla soup can be thought of as a fusion of sorts and not really a traditional recipe. The big difference in their recipe is that instead of the bean infused thick soup that other Mexican / Spanish restaurants serve, this is actually very delicately flavoured soup with a clear broth. Light refreshing and yumm! this is my go to place when I crave some chicken tortilla soup. Not sure if this qualifies as the authentic deal as it lacks beans, but I really don't care as it is delicious nevertheless. Here is my attempt at replicating the Soho chicken tortilla soup.

Ingredients

20 min   **4 ppl**

Chicken broth: 4 cups

Chicken: 1cup (boneless, skinless chicken breasts boiled and shredded)

Cheese: ½ cup Monterey Jack or Parmesan

Avocado: 1 large

Tomatoes: 1 large cut into one inch cubes

Sweet corn: ½ cup par boiled or grilled

Tortilla: 2 - cut into thin strips and toasted (You can also use the store bought tortillas.)

Lime juice: 3 tbsps

Dhania (Coriander) leaves for garnish: 10 tender stems chopped fine

Salt: 1-2 tsp as per taste

Red Chilli flakes for garnish: 1 tsp

Method

1. Bring the chicken broth to boil with the tomatoes (10 minutes)
2. Remove from fire, mash the tomatoes and strain, discarding the tomato skin and seeds etc.
3. Bring back to heat and boil.
4. Add the shredded chicken and tomatoes, reduce heat. Simmer on medium heat for 5 minutes.
5. Add corn and lime and simmer for 5 more minutes. Remove from heat and add lime juice.
6. Cut the avocadoes into medium sized wedges. Keep aside.
7. In 4 soup bowls portion and add cheese. Pour equal amounts of the soup on the cheese.
8. Put in a wedge of avocado in each soup bowl. Sprinkle coriander leaves and tortilla strips on top and serve immediately.

Note:
The soup tastes really well with grilled corn. You can either grill the corn or roast the frozen corn in a little bit of oil in a pan and then use it in the soup. Tortillas are first smeared with a little oil, cut into strips and roasted in an oven @ 200 degree for 5 -7 minutes to get the nice crunchy garnish for this soup.

FRENCH ONION SOUP
Browned onion soup

Soups range from clear to creamy to thick vegetable chowders that are nutritious, filling and meals by themselves. They warm the body and comfort the soul. Soup remains popular among dieters and foodies alike. Though technically an appetizer, it can be tweaked to make a main course dish.

When the mercury drops they start to make an appearance on my dining table and then continue to hold fort all through the winter months. They are simple to prepare, tasty and with a little bit of imagination (and creativity) you can make several variations. A soup and sandwich combo is also way easier to put together (with fewer dirty dishes at the end) than most other meals. With stock cubes being easily available making soups is only a matter of minutes. However making your own stock- be it vegetarian or chicken is far more rewarding.

French onion soup is a variation of the classic French onion soup. It is a rich tasting soup with melt in the mouth onions. Served piping hot and with accompaniments like warm, buttered toast or garlic bread.

Ingredients

Onions: 3, finely chopped (Some prefer it sliced)

Butter: 2 tbsps

Chicken stock: 4/5 cups(To prepare chicken stock, pressure cook 3 or 4 bony chicken pieces with 6-8 cups of water, quartered onions, some whole pepper and salt for about 20 minutes. Strain and use the water)

Grated cheese: 6 tbsps

Corn flour: 2 tsps

Sabut Kali mirch (Whole Pepper) crushed: 2

Chopped parsley (optional): 2 tsps

Salt and pepper to taste

 30 mins   4 ppl

Method

1. Heat the butter and fry the onions on low flame for 10/15 minutes until golden brown in colour.

2. Add the stock, salt and pepper and bring it to a boil.

3. Mix the corn flour in about a cup of water and add to the soup. Simmer for 5 minutes.

4. Make little balls with the grated cheese, crushed peppercorns and chopped parsley (if using) and drop them into the soup just before serving.

5. Serve hot.

Note:
Cooking the onions for a very long time over low heat mellows their flavour. Make sure you don't stir too often as then the onions won't caramelize. Tastes best with home-made chicken stock.

PUDINA SHERBET
Mint, lemon and ginger drink

Sherbets by definition are concentrates to which you add water or soda. I come from a generation that grew up on sherbets and squashes. No packaged juice and aerated drinks beat a hasty treat in the late 70's to re-enter India much later. Most common among all was orange squash. Prepared, stocked and served in everybody's home.

My fondest memory around this drink is during holi. Holi, the festival of colours, also marked the beginning of summer. Growing up in a small town where we had lived for years meant that it was a community event. The day would start with all the uncles (yes, which is how we referred to our neighbours and any friends of our parents) in their dazzling white churidar kurtas going from one house to the next (we referred to it as 'colony' though row houses maybe a more familiar word today). Gaining in strength (literally) as they gathered and herded everybody together. The women usually joined in a little later. We saw a more fun side to the elders that day. Lot of hugging (which they otherwise did not), screaming 'bura na mano holi hai' (meaning everything goes today) and loud, unrestrained laughter. We would wait expectantly for the crowd to reach our house. After the colour exchange was done the guests (they didn't feel like guests on Holi- given the camaraderie) would be served orange squash and meetha boondi (a type of sweet). We would manage to quietly sneak a glass each time we had a new set of visitors. If more people arrived that expected water or ice got added to the squash but in the spirit of Holi nobody seemed to mind the diluted version. The crowd would then merge at the local Club (the high point of our life). People would sing, dance and be merry. The songs would range from traditional folk ones like 'rangwa daro na sawariyan mano humari' to 'rang barse' which used to be the most popular bollywood holi number and stayed on top of the charts for years. Holi made for some happy times and fond memories.

Mom continues to make sherbets especially the pudina (mint) one during the hot summer months. Usually with fresh mint leaves from her garden. I end up settling for a ready to drink version most of the times. But occasionally I do take the effort and a short emotional trip down my childhood lane.

Ingredients

Pudina (Mint) leaves: 1 cup
Sugar: 1 cup
Water: 1 cup
Ginger: 1 inch, grated
Lime juice: ½ tsp per glass while serving

15 mins   6 ppl

Method

1. Heat the water and sugar together. Stir till the sugar dissolves completely.

2. Next add the pudina and ginger and simmer for a few minutes only. Just enough time for the flavours to infuse.

3. Switch off the gas stove and let the syrup cool down. Strain and store in the refrigerator in a clean glass bottle.

4. To serve, mix one part concentrate with two parts water, ½ tsp lime juice and some ice cubes. Garnish with a sprig of mint and a slice of lime.

5. Enjoy this refreshing summer cooler drink. You could also add one part of the concentrate to your regular nimboo pani (lemonade) to give it a creative twist.

LEMON GINGER COOLER
Sweet and spicy lemon drink

I just love ginger. When I cook I find ginger spices up any daal, meat or even curries very delicately. Aromatic, pungent and spicy, ginger adds a special flavour and zest to stir fries as well. Its health benefits are numerous. Due to its anti-inflammatory properties, ginger is medically speaking truly a super food. As an added bonus, fresh ginger root is conveniently available year round in the produce section of your local market.
Usually found in savoury dishes, ginger is a sort of late entrant to sweet dishes. Now of course it is commonplace to find ginger cookies and ginger breads and cakes. While savoury dishes mask the strong ginger tang, sweet dishes heighten the flavours and aroma. In this drink, there is no masking. If you love ginger, this is a great drink for you.

Ingredients

30 mins   8 ppl

Ginger: 6 medium to large roots, grated
Sugar: 1cup
Kali Mirch (Black pepper): 1/2 tsp
Lemon: 1 medium sized
Salt: 1/2 tsp
Water: 3 cups
Ice Cubes: 6

Method

1. Remove the skin and grate the ginger. You will need about a cup of grated ginger

2. In a heavy bottom pan boil the water and add the ginger to it. Continue on medium heat for about 10 minutes, till the water reduces to about half.

3. Add sugar and continue to stir on medium heat till the sugar dissolves completely (about 5 minutes).

4. Make sure that the sugar doesn't harden or crystalize.

5. Remove from fire and wait till the mixture is completely cool.

6. Add ice cubes, black pepper, salt and blend in a mixer for a minute.

7. Strain the mixture and store in a bottle.

8. When you are ready to serve, pour the mixture in a glass till about half full. Squeeze some lemon juice and stir.

9. Garnish with a lemon twist and serve with crushed ice.

Note:
This drink has a spicy kick to it and can be made ahead of time. It can be refrigerated and stays fresh for up to weeks. I have added vodka to it and also served it as a cocktail. You can adjust the sugar to taste. You can also freeze this drink in an ice cube tray and serve the flavoured cubes later with other drinks like regular nimboo pani or even coke, to add an unusual flavour.

SAAR
An Indian tomato soup with coconut milk

My Uncle (Kaka- Dad's younger brother) introduced me to Saar. He has probably forgotten all about it now but oh well. I had just finished my graduation exams and was essentially whiling my time waiting for the results to be out. So I decided to go up to Delhi and spend about a month with them and my niece who was two year old then. Quite a gourmet cook himself, in spite of being a busy surgeon, Kaka did make a couple of dishes from time to time when I was there. One day he announced with a flourish that he would be making "Saar". I had no clue what it was and I thought it was some kind of inspiration from his Marathi friends. After a while we were served with what looked to me like plain old tomato soup. But once I had the first spoonful, I realized that it was much more than just tomato soup. Although I didn't know how it was made or what the ingredients were, I still remember the rich taste and flavours that made this probably the best kind of tomato soup you can have. Later on I got the recipe from some friends and tweaked it to my taste. Till date it remains my favourite tomato soup...if you can call it that. I think it is much more.

Ingredients

20 mins   **4-6 ppl**

For the Soup:
- Tomatoes: 6, medium cut into wedges
- Curry leaves: 10 leaves
- Coconut milk: ½ cup
- Urad daal (Black gram) split: 1tbsp
- Ginger: 1 inch, grated
- Mustard seeds: 1tbsp

For the Tadka:
- Green Chillies: 1
- Hing (Asafoetida): 1 tsp
- Sugar: 1 tsp (Optional)
- Red chilli flakes: ½ tsp
- Water: 3 cups
- Oil: 1 tbsp (Vegetable oil)

Method

1. Boil tomatoes in 3 cups of water, green chillies and grated ginger for about 10 minutes.
2. Remove from fire and cool.
3. Blend tomato mixture in a blender for about a minute and then quickly strain to remove seeds and skin. What you will now get is slightly dense spicy tomato purée.
4. In a kadai/wok, heat some oil and add the curry leaves.
5. Almost immediately add the dal and the mustard seeds and the red chili flakes.
6. When the mustard seeds begin to splutter, add the asafoetida powder, tomato purée and coconut milk.
7. Bring to a quick boil.
8. Remove from fire and add the sugar and salt to taste. Serve hot.

Note:
This soup is spicy and rich. Although fresh ingredients taste the best, one can also use canned tomatoes and canned coconut milk if fresh ingredients are not at hand.

MANGO LASSI
A rich, sweet, mango flavoured yogurt drink

Growing up in India, I used to wait for summers so I could eat mangoes. In many parts of the world, mango is classified as an exotic fruit. To me, mango was as commonplace as it could get. In fact, I grew up thinking strawberries or peaches were the exotic fruits. Mango is seen in the Indian grocery stores only during the summer months. We used to get sack loads of the fruit, in various stages of ripeness, from my grandfather's village. My grandmother used to painstakingly make a bed of sand and the fruits would be neatly arranged in a rectangular matrix on the sand bed and allowed to ripen at room temperature for many days before we could eat them. All of our cousins used to gather at our grandfather's home for the summers. Every morning, all of us cousins would gather around the mangoes, test them for ripeness and only the most squishy, ripe ones that smelt fruity enough would make it to the lunch table as a refreshing desert at the end of a hearty, summer meal. The ones that were over ripe would invariably end up as 'lassi'. Times have changed now and one can easily find cans of mango pulp in almost every part of the world. Like most recipes, this drink tastes the best with fresh mango pulp. But using mango pulp from a can tastes equally good and is much more convenient to use. This lassi is very filling and great on a hot summer day.... irrespective of whichever part of the world you live in.

Ingredients

Sweetened Mango Pulp: 1 cup
Unflavoured Curd (Yogurt): ½ cup
Sugar: 2 tbsps
Low fat milk: ¼ cup
Crushed ice: 1 cup

10 mins   2 ppl

Method

1. Whisk all the ingredients in a blender and serve immediately.

Note:
Freshly cut mangoes or crushed almonds are great garnishes for this drink.

WATERMELON COOLER
Refreshing summer drink with watermelons

Every time I think of Watermelons, visions of Indian summers come to mind. Indian summers are hot, humid and just unbearable at times. We had to really come up with innovative ways of staying cool. Although aerated drinks were available, they were reserved for some special events or when one ate out in restaurants. Fruit based homemade drinks like mango lassi, aam panna, nimboo pani were summer staples in India. Watermelons were sold stacked up near the roadside usually with a couple of them cut and on display to show how "red" the inside was. If the vendor was nice, he would even offer a small wedge for you to sample. It was also a skill to choose a ripe watermelon that was juicy and sweet. The darker the skins, the sweeter they were. The watermelons those days had big black seeds in them. We used to cut them in slices and devour the sweet juicy flesh sitting out in the backyard, the sun blazing down our heads and spitting out the seeds at regular intervals. Later on, the seedless variety made its entry and one has to thank genetic engineering for making some things easier. This recipe combines ginger and lemon to create a nice, bold cocktail. The best part about the drink is its bright pinkish red colour which is almost unnatural in its brightness.

Ingredients

Watermelon: 1 medium (preferably seedless)
Ginger: 1 inch, grated
Sugar: 4 tsps. (Optional)
Kali Mirch (Black pepper): 1/4th tsp.
Pudina (Mint): 10 leaves
Lemon: 1 medium sized
Salt: 1/4th tsp.
Ice Cubes: 6

10 mins   2 ppl

Method

1. Remove the flesh of the watermelon taking care to remove any visible seeds.

2. Blend the Watermelon till it is well mashed and liquid in texture. (About 1 minute on high speed)

3. Add the ginger, sugar, black pepper, salt, ice cubes and half of the mint leaves and blend again for about a minute.

4. Squeeze the juice of one lemon into the mixture and mix well.

5. Strain the mixture into 4 tall glasses. Garnish with the remaining mint leaves and serve immediately.

Note:
This drink tastes best when made fresh and served immediately. To make things easier you can cut the watermelon about 2 hours ahead of time and make it when the guests start arriving. You can also add some vodka to spike this drink and make an exotic cocktail out of it.

CHICKEN LARB
A cold refreshing Thai Salad

As a family we love Thai food. But sometimes my daughters find it too spicy. One of my daughters is addicted to the Food Network Channel and discovered chicken larb by accident. She watched Giada de Laurentiis demonstrate chicken larb on a show and was desperate to try it. So at our next Thai dinner, sure enough, larb chicken was what she ordered. I really hadn't noticed the dish on the menu but to my surprise, almost every Thai restaurant in town features this dish. Interestingly, it tastes different in every restaurant. Soon after, I started experimenting with larb in my own kitchen. My first attempt at larb was Giada's recipe (turkey larb) where I substituted the turkey with chicken. Kids loved it! I personally found it both a little too tangy and too sweet for my palette. Next time I tweaked a few ingredients to her recipe and the results were more in tune with my taste. I kept experimenting till I found my perfect recipe for larb.

Larb makes an ideal appetizer for pool or BBQ parties. You can also make this beforehand and since it is served at room temperature, it weathers quite well left out in the open for outdoor events. Unlike traditional salads, this recipe calls for serving the larb with cabbage leaves instead of lettuce, which is an advantage in summers as cabbage wilts a lot later than lettuce.

Ingredients

20 mins   4-6 ppl

For the Larb
Grated chicken: 2 cups
Red onions: - ½ cup, finely chopped
Small onions (Shallots): 1/4th cup, chopped
Olive oil/ Vegetable oil: 2 tbsps
Pudina (Mint) leaves: ½ cup, chopped
Green chilies: 2, julienned
Kali mirch (Pepper): ¼ tsp crushed
Salt: 1 Tsp or to taste
Cabbage: 1 small (cut into half, leaves separated into large "bowls" for serving the larb)

For the Dressing
Fresh Lemon/ Lime juice: 4 tbsps.
Honey: 1tbsp.
Dhania (Coriander) leaves: 2 tbsps., finely chopped
Fish sauce: 1tbsp.

Method

1. Take all the ingredients for the dressing in a bowl. Whisk them together and keep aside.

2. In a large skillet, heat the oil and add the onions, shallots and cook till they soften (about 3 to 4 minutes).

3. Add the grated chicken and the mint. Cook for about 7 minutes on medium heat, till the chicken is almost done. Season with salt and pepper.

4. Add the dressing and cook for 3 more minutes.

5. Line the cabbage bowls on a serving platter..

6. Spoon the chicken onto the cabbage bowls and serve.

Note:
- You can use Turkey instead of chicken.
- While cooking the chicken, stir to make sure that the chicken turns out crumbly

CARROT AND RAISIN SALAD
Refreshing and flavoursome summer salad

Modern day salads have repositioned the category. People today opt for salads by choice, for their taste and not because they have been asked to go easy on oil or spice as the case used to be. So much so that a popular women's magazine had a salad supplement with its last issue, as many as 100 salads, many of them modified to suit the Indian palate.

From being prepared with basic vegetables like cucumber, tomato, onion(radish, carrot and beet root added in the winter months) salads have graduated to ones with more exotic names like tossed rice salad, lentil salads, pina colada salad. We have started to think more innovatively when preparing our salads. I for one, keep adding newer ingredients even after I have started making the salad. If serving salad as a meal, I typically add bread croutons or a handful of boiled pasta to give more body to the salad. Handy when you are entertaining with no last minute bother of heating or frying. Keep the ingredients ready, toss them all together and serve. Most salads can be prepared way ahead and served chilled. Keep a little bit of the seasoning handy in case all of it gets absorbed.

This carrot and raisin salad uses orange juice, lime juice, freshly ground cumin, crushed garlic and honey as the dressing. Goes really well with fiery curries. Tastes wonderful and can be carried over to the next day without losing out on taste or crunchiness.

Ingredients

30 mins   4 ppl

Carrots: 500 grams, julienned (cut into matchstick like pieces, do not grate)
Raisins: 10
Roasted peanut: 2 tbsps, lighted crushed
Orange juice: ½ cup
Lime juice: 2 tbsps
Garlic: 3 pods, crushed
Roasted and powdered Jeera (Cumin): 1 tsp
Toasted Til(Sesame) seeds: 2 tsps
Dhania (Coriander) leaves: 2 tbsps
Honey: 1 tsp
Salt and pepper to taste

Method

1. Steam the carrots for a minute or two (if the carrots are tender you could skip this stage) and refresh in ice cold water. Drain the water.

2. Soak the raisins in warm water for about 10/15 minutes to plump them up.

3. Mix together the orange juice, lime juice, garlic, jeera powder, honey, dhania leaves, salt and pepper and give it a good whisk. Pour over the carrots, add the raisins and let the salad chilli in the refrigerator for a couple of hours. The carrots will absorb all the flavours from the dressing.

4. Mix the sesame seeds and peanuts right before serving so that they retain their crunch

Note:
Salads have indeed come a long way, they are no longer an apology on the side. This salad uses multiple ingredients that add flavour. Do make sure you get the proportions and balance right. So keep tasting the dressing and tweaking it as necessary.

KHAMANG KAKDI
Tempered, crunchy cucumber salad

I discovered this dish just a few years ago. I came across a variation of the recipe in a women's magazine, as I was getting a spa pedicure done. As I was in no state to write the recipe down, made a note to get home and search for it on the Internet. It turned out to be pretty simple actually. I later learnt that it was a popular Maharashtrian (Western India) cucumber salad. Now, cucumber is a regular salad ingredient in most households- cut into roundels and served along with onion and tomatoes. Sometimes, cubed and served with the same set of ingredients. But 'khamang kakdi', thanks to the tempering, manages to elevate the ubiquitous cucumber to a different level.

The 'desi tadka' (local Indian tempering) technically takes the dish out of what Indians call the salad category (read bland, tasteless, a 'peripheral' dish unless you are on a diet). This one is bursting with flavours- tangy, sweet, spicy and more. It is so good that you can have it plain, without a main course accompanying it.

It is a refreshing, cool salad and more popular during the hot summer months. It also helps balance the heavier flavours of richer curries in the meal. Since discovering 'khamang kakdi', this is the only way I like my cucumber salad.

Ingredients

30 mins   **4 ppl**

Cucumbers: 2
Grated coconut: 3 tbsps
Lemon juice: 3 tbsp (one lemon should suffice)
Sugar: 1 tsp
Salt: 1 tsp
Oil: 1 tsp

Mustard seeds: 2 tsp
Curry leaves: 1 sprig (20 leaves)
Peanuts: Fistful (roasted and crushed)
Green chillies: 1, finely chopped
Dhania (Coriander) leaves: 2 tbsps, finely chopped

Method

1. Cube the cucumbers; leave the skin on for both goodness and taste.

2. Add sugar and salt to the lime juice. Mix well. It will take a couple of minutes for the sugar to dissolve completely. Be patient. Add this juice to the cubed cucumbe

3. Next add the grated coconut, chopped coriander, green chillies, and crushed peanuts to the cucumber.

4. Mix well.

5. Heat some oil in a kadhai (wok). Once the oil heats up, add the mustard seeds and let them sputter. Then add the curry leaves and toss around for half a minute. Let this cool down a bit.

6. Add the tempering to the salad and chill. Serve cold along with rice and a spicy curry.

7. Serve immediately.

Note:
The roasted and crushed peanuts, freshly grated coconut, mustard and curry leaf combine give this delicious but simple recipe its unique flavour. It also works well as a refreshing, light food between meals.

MANGO KALE SPROUT SALAD
Summer salad with the new super food – Kale!

I discovered kale in California. I was visiting Radha and Vivek in Palo Alto for an impromptu reunion of the "Dairy Farm" when another friend of ours - Lyn was visiting. There is a long story about why we were called the "Dairy Farm" during our college days, which will probably feature in my memoirs and not in this cookbook. Nevertheless it was a great weekend catching up with college friends after nearly twenty two years. Bhamans the ever gracious hosts had whipped up, among other things, a dry curry made of kale and potatoes. At first I mistook it for spinach. When I dug into the curry, I realized that the leaves were a little harder and had a very different taste that I instantly liked; much better than spinach. Although I had heard of kale, I tried it for the first time at their home. I came back to Atlanta and immediately started scouting around for kale leaves. I realized that they were easily available in grocery stores all around the US. The following summer, I started experimenting with kale a lot making chips, salads and also adding it with lentils and using it for typical Indian recipes. One of the healthiest vegetables you can find, a high concentration of vitamin A and potassium combined with a very low glycemic load (3),and an abundance of anti-inflammatory properties makes kale a nutritionist's delight.

This recipe uses baby kale which is tenderer than the other varieties and works well in salads and other dishes where it is used in the raw form.

Ingredients

10 mins   6 ppl

Kale: 4 cups

Semi ripe mangoes cut into small cubes: 1 cup

Moong (Green gram) sprouts: 1 cup

Jeera (Cumin) seeds roasted and ground: 1 tbsp

Olive oil: 2 tbsps

Dhania (Coriander) leaves chopped: ½ cup

Ginger paste: 1 tsp

Fresh Lemon Juice: 3 tbsps

Amchoor (Dry mango powder) 1 tbsp

Kali Mirch (Black pepper) ground: 1/2 tsp

Salt: 1/2 tsp

Sugar: ¼ tsp

Method

1. In a bowl mix lemon juice olive oil and ginger paste till well blended.

2. Add sugar, salt, pepper, amchoor and jeera powder and mix well to make the dressing.

3. Add mango, kale and moong sprouts till well coated with the dressing.

4. Serve right away.

Note:
You can roast about half a cup of cumin seeds and grind to make and store the powder ahead of time. The excess powder can be used for other dishes later. For making sprouts at home, soak whole green moong seeds overnight. In the morning put the seeds into a thin muslin cloth and tie tightly. Keep aside for a day or two to get nice long sprouted moong.

Here in the US I just wrap the soaked moong in a paper kitchen towel and leave it for two days.

PINACORN SALAD
Vegetable salad in a light mayo dressing

"What's in a name?" I am sorry but this Shakespearian logic definitely does not extend to food. The more complex the dish sounds, the more intrigued you are about its taste. So, if you were to tell your friends that you were making 'Moussaka', the response would be, "wow!" And then, quickly followed by, "hey, but what is that?" Would the dish have had a similar impact, had you, for example said, "I am making Keema Alu baigan" (mince with potato and aubergine which are the key ingredients of moussaka)?

When it comes to naming their dishes, the French take the cake. Crème Brule, Mango Gateaux, Crepes Screes and so it goes. But, unless you are French or into food, when dining at a restaurant, you are more likely to call the steward, point to the dish on the menu card and say, "I want one of that." The Mughals too, tempt you with names like Nargisi Kofta, Dum Murg, Murg Noorjehani, Shahi Kaju Aloo. Prefix any dish with 'Shahi' which means royal, and it does sound like a 'dainty dish to be set before a king'.

It was at a cousin's place that I first sampled this corn salad. The salad looked interesting, tasted really nice but it was the name that finally did the trick. It was called Pinacorn salad. There was an exotic feel to the name, a certain lilt to it. So some quick sms exchanges, some searches, a few tweaks later, the dish made its way to our dinner table.

Ingredients

15 mins   4 ppl

Sweet Corn: 200 gms

Tinned Pineapple slices: 2 to 3, cubed

Cherry Tomatoes: 8 to10

Walnuts: 3 to 4 crushed

Lettuce: 1 bunch

Paneer(Cottage cheese cubed): 50 gms

Thousand Island dressing: 2 to 3 tbsp

Method

1. Boil the sweet corn.
2. Mix all the ingredients together.
3. Layer the serving dish with lettuce.
4. Serve the salad on this bed of lettuce.

Note:
A great tasting salad, without the usual mess of peeling and chopping. To make this a complete meal, you could also add a handful of boiled pasta and some blanched tender beans.

Snacks and Starters

DAHIBARA ALUDAM GHUGUNI
A staple east indian street food

Let me start with a simple food quiz. Have you heard of the following?
Dahi bara/Dahi wada- Yes/No? Alu dam- Yes/No? Ghuguni/Patiala Matar/Matra- Yes/No? Most of you would I am sure have got a yes for all three. Now for the clincher, Dahi wada+ Alu dam+ Ghuguni all served as a snack combo- familiar? How many Non-Odias got a yes to the last one? If you did, then you are definitely in the minority. And I can safely assume that either you have good Odia friends and have been subjected to Odia hospitality or have travelled to Odisha, more specifically to Cuttack, where this used to be the most popular snack. I say used to be because, today it is no longer just a snack. It has replaced every possible meal. People start and end their day with this combo. You are never too full for ADDB (Alu dam dahi bara). So before, after, in between meals. When you are hungry and also after you are stuffed.

People from Cuttack are crazy about their alu dam dahi bara. And don't you dare dismiss this off as mere street food. The brand name plays a big part here. There are clear camps- the ones who like the 'Raghu' brand and there are others who prefer brand 'Bhagi'. These are individuals who have been making and selling ADDB for generations. They enjoy semi-god like status and have Facebook pages dedicated to them. Each camp defends their brand very strongly. Reminds me of the East Bengal- Mohan Bagan warring groups one came across in Kolkata- yes, the same level of passion and enthusiasm. And NEVER ever attempt passing one brand for the other (the loyalists are quick to identify the brand even visually when sent as a photograph- I can vouch for this). ADDB is carried from Cuttack to various parts of the country and across continents (this is no exaggeration). The die-hards of course insist that it is not the same as eating the ones made at home. As for me, I started with a lot of scepticism- dahi bara with alu dam (why not with the regular imli chutney as the rest of the country enjoys it). Let me quickly clarify that I liked all three (dahi bara, alu dam and ghuguni) and used to eat them separately with other accompaniments. So dahi bara with imli chutney, alu dam with paratha/ puri and ghuguni again with paratha or puri or roti. I did not see any sense in mixing all of them into this hotchpotch. And then slowly over the years I grew to like it (maybe it is an acquired taste- you acquire it when you marry somebody from Cuttack). And now, I am a complete convert. Though, I am still not brand loyal (forgive me Raghu/Bhagi), but yes a trip to Cuttack does not seem complete without a plate of ADDB. Usually happens to be my first meal (but that must just be a coincidence).

I have also been making it quite regularly at home and have been introducing a lot of our friends to the combination. It is only a matter of time before ADDB gains popularity and starts selling as street food across the country. I would be happy to have played a small part in its journey.

Ingredients

soaking time: 5-6 hrs 60 mins 6 ppl

For the Dahi bara
- Urad daal (White lentil): 1 cup, soak for 2 to 3 hours
- Ginger: 1 tsp, finely chopped
- Green chillies: finely chopped
- Salt: to taste
- Oil: for frying

For the Alu Dam
- Baby potatoes: 300 grams
- Whole jeera (Cumin): 1 tsp
- Dhania (Coriander) powder: 1½ tsps
- Jeera (Cumin) powder: 1 tsp
- Tomato: 2 (grated)
- Salt: to taste
- Garam masala: a pinch
- Oil: 2 tbsps
- Water: 2 cups

For the Ghuguni
- Ghuguni matar: 1 cup (also goes by the name Patiala matar or Matra) soak for 5-6 hours
- Jeera (Cumin): 1 tsp
- Dhania (Coriander): 1 tsp
- Ginger: 1 inch, ground to a paste
- Garlic: 5 pods, ground to a paste
- Salt to taste
- Tomatoes: 2
- Oil: 1 tbsp

For the garnish
- Onion: 1, finely chopped
- Green chillies: 2 to 3, finely chopped
- Chilli powder: to taste
- Roasted Jeera(Cumin) powder: to taste
- Cuttack mixture: 2 tsps per serve

Garam masala can be prepared by grinding equal portions of dalchini(cinnamon), elaichi(cardamom), laung(clove) and kali mirch(whole Pepper) to a fine powder. Proportion and ingredients could vary by region.

Method

You make all the three parts separately and then assemble them together like a chaat.

Dahi bara

1. Grind the soaked urad daal with a little bit of water to a fine paste. Add the salt, ginger and chillies and mix well.

2. Heat some oil and drop the urad batter into it like small balls. Once the baras are done drop them into hot water and let them rest there for a while (about 10 minutes).

3. Remove the baras, squeeze them between your palms and keep them on a plate.

4. Mix the dahi with some water, salt, chilli powder, roasted and ground cumin and red chilli powder. Pour over the baras. Please note that the dahi is of a much thinner consistency than the North Indian version.

Alu dam

5. Boil the potatoes and remove the skin.

6. Heat the oil and add the whole jeera to it. Once the jeera browns, add the boiled potatoes and fry them for a bit. Add the salt. Make a paste by mixing the jeera and dhania powder with a little bit of water and add to the potatoes. Next, add the tomatoes and approximately about 2 cups of water. Finally, add the garam masala.

Ghuguni

7. Boil the ghuguni and keep aside.

8. Heat the oil and fry all the masala. Add the boiled ghuguni. Adjust the water so that you get a 'makha makha' (semi-liquid) consistency.

To assemble

10. Layer the bowl or plate with some dahi bara, then add the alu dam and ghuguni. Garnish with onion, green chillies, chilli powder, roasted jeera powder and mixture.

11. Serve immediately. Dig in

Note:

Take a bow at having mastered this elaborate dish. Make sure to thank Raghu, Bhagi and all the people from Cuttack.

FISH CUTLETS
Bite sized fish patties

My memory has served me well so far. Sis says "I may forgive but I never forget". And if it's got to do with food, then you can be sure I will carry the memory to my grave. Fondest among these are my mother's fish cutlets- they were melt in the mouth and to die for. She made them with all types of fish. In fact very often, with tuna a fish that most others turned up their noses at. Mom would first get our household help to fillet the tuna, then she would sauté them with some garlic to get rid of the fishy smell and several steps later they would appear on our dinner table as the most delicious cutlets garnished with some onion rings and lime wedges. Winter evenings we had them along with soup and bread.

Mom taught me how to make fish cutlets. I was amazed at how simple the steps were. That did not take away from the taste. Mom also made them with very little oil which I guess makes them healthy. We now have cutlets as regulars on our menu. Convenient as starters, go well as meal accompaniments, eaten as evening snacks, leftovers get converted into sandwich/burger filling.

Ingredients

 60 mins   6-8 ppl

- Fish: 3 to 4 pieces (Stomach portion with fewer bones or 200 grams of Fillet)
- Onions: 2 medium sized ones, chopped really fine
- Pudina (Mint leaves): handful, finely chopped
- Oil: 2 tbsp
- Ginger: 1", finely chopped
- Potatoes: 2 to 3 boiled
- Bread crumbs: 2 to 3 tbsps. to coat cutlets
- Dhania(Coriander)leaves: 2 tbsp finely chopped
- Haldi(Turmeric): 1 tsp
- Salt: To taste
- Green chillies (optional): 2 to 3

Method

1. Smear salt and turmeric on the fish pieces and shallow fry them in 1 teaspoon oil. Debone the fish.

2. Heat about 2 teaspoons of oil. Fry the onion till glassy, add the ginger and sauté for a few more minutes. Next add the fish and cook together for about 5 minutes.

3. Remove from fire, add boiled potatoes, bread crumbs, some finely chopped green chillies (if using), the mint and coriander leaves and mix well. Make small round balls with the mixture and flatten lightly between your palms.

4. Spread the remaining bread crumbs on a plate and place the cutlets over them. Turn the cutlets around so that the crumbs coat them evenly.

5. Heat a teaspoon of oil in a non-stick, shallow pan. Once the oil heats up, add the cutlets one by one. Arrange them on the pan and fry on both sides.

6. Serve hot, garnished with some onion rings, lemon wedges and a chutney/dip.

Note:
Thank you Mama, for this wonderful recipe. Helps me relive a part of my childhood, with each bite.

QUINOA UPMA
Spicy, hearty quinoa with vegetables

I recently discovered a new grain called Quinoa (pronounced keen-wa). A friend suggested that I try it and once I bought a pack of quinoa home, I was sufficiently curious to find out more. Turns out, quinoa's origins are truly ancient. It was one of the three staple foods, along with corn and potatoes, of the Inca civilization. Quinoa was known then, and still is known, with respect, as the mother grain. Nutritionists call it the 'super grain of the future.' This is because, quinoa contains more protein than any other grain; an average of 16.2 percent, with some varieties containing as much as 20%. The grain has an interesting texture. It looks like a micro mini mustard seed but when you cook it, it splits to reveal a small threadlike texture tight in the middle of the quinoa grain. Nutty in texture, quinoa by itself doesn't have a distinct flavour. This makes it the perfect raw material for many dishes, as it has the ability to take on the flavour of all the ingredients you choose to add with it.

I thought of trying out a traditional Indian dish called 'Upma', which is usually made with semolina or cream of wheat. I substituted the traditional ingredients with quinoa and the results were surprisingly good. So here it is....

Ingredients

Quinoa: 1 cup
Onion: 1 large finely chopped
Green chilly: 1 small finely chopped
Mixed vegetables, chopped into small pieces: 1 cup (I used carrots, peas and beans)
Olive oil: 1 tbsp

Water: 2 cups
For the garnish
Mustard seeds: 1 tsp
Curry leaves: 10
Cashew nuts: 6 to 8
Tomato: 1 slice

 60 mins   4 ppl

Method

1. Wash the quinoa. Take 2 cups of water and use the rice cooker to cook the quinoa. Quinoa can also be cooked in a sauce pan, the same way you would cook rice.

2. In a separate wok, heat 1 tablespoon olive oil and put the green chillies and onions. Sauté the onions till they look transparent.

3. Add the vegetables and cook till they are 3/4th done. Mix in the cooked quinoa with the vegetables over low heat. Remove from fire.

4. In a separate pan, melt a spoon of clarified butter and put the curry leaves and the mustard seeds till they start sputtering.

5. Add the cashews and sauté till the cashews are nice and golden brown in colour.

6. In a separate wok, heat 1 tablespoon olive oil and put the green chillies and onions. Sauté the onions till they look transparent.

7. I used a wine glass to serve it in and garnished it with a slice of tomato. If you are going to do this and get all fancy, suggest using warm and not piping hot upma as the glass may break.

Note:
- You can use any vegetable oil instead of Olive oil.
- This dish is best eaten hot.
- Skip the chilly if you don't want the dish to be very spicy.

SESAME POTATOES
Crispy, crunchy potatoes with sesame seeds

Get me started on starters and I could just go on. There is just something about those bite-sized finger foods that get me all excited. When we get invited for a meal, my focus of attention is always the stuff that precedes the main meal. Appetizers are the perfect way to begin a meal. Starters also allow for a lot of creative play and experimentation. They range from plain basic mixtures (deep fried savoury mix) to pan-seared chicken tikkas.

If you are making three or four starters, which is how it usually is, you need a mix of light and heavy starters; some that can be made early on like a cheese and pineapple stick and others which need to be fried and served hot. Large bowls of salads or fresh, cut fruits can also be served alongside or left in small bowls around the room.

I first heard about sesame potatoes from my bhabi (sister-in-law). She in turn had sampled it at a friend's place. I cajoled her to get me the recipe and very soon I was making my variant of it. It now enjoys a permanent spot on my entertainment menu. Quick, easy and flavoursome. And goes well with almost any other starter that you plan to serve.

Ingredients

30 mins   6-8 ppl

Baby potatoes: 300 grams

Til (Sesame) seeds: 3 tbsps., roasted

Oil: 2 tbsps

Oregano seasoning: 1 tsp (you could also use one or two of the leftover pizza seasoning sachets, works very well)

Chilli flakes: 1 tsp (optional)

Salt: 1 tsp

Method

1. Wash and prick the baby potatoes with a toothpick. Boil them in some salt water for about 10/15 minutes. They should be completely cooked but firm. Alternatively you can also pressure cook them for one whistle and let the cooker cool down naturally.

2. Next heat oil in a kadai/wok. Add the baby potatoes and turn them around. Sauté on high flame for a couple of minutes so that the potatoes get crisp on the outside.

3. Next add the sesame seeds, oregano and chilli flakes (if using) so that the seasoning coats the potatoes.

4. Remove and serve hot as a starter on toothpicks.

Note:
Ideally serve with a spicy dip. There are multiple variations of this recipe. You could substitute oregano with some bhuna jeera (roasted cumin), add some roasted and crushed peanuts, add some fried garlic flakes, drizzle the potatoes with some spicy chutney. Potato especially in this form is very versatile. Even goes well as a main course accompaniment (though it needs to be cooked when the guests are ready for the meal).

PAO BHAJI
Spicy vegetable dish served with hot buns

Pao bhaji is one dish that I did not grow up eating. It is Mumbai's hottest selling street food and that is how I got initiated into trying it. My office in Mumbai was in the heart of a busy commercial area. The street vendors made brisk business during lunch time. Most people stepped down from those tall towers to grab a quick bite and a little bit of that fresh sea breeze before heading back for another long haul. These stalls would be packed with people but the vendor would still manage to customize as per your requirement- extra onions or no butter or loads of butter as the case might have been. I loved the way they would have the bhaji cooked from earlier and stacked in a ring around the large pan. After you had placed your order, they would fry a little bit of it in butter and dish it out to you. The choice of garnish included green coriander, finely chopped onions, a slice of lime, some green chillies and a dollop of butter. The butter melting as the chap handed over your plate, the aroma of melted butter mmmmm! You then dipped hot, buttered buns that were served alongside, into the bhaji and relished each mouthful.

For me, pao bhaji is more than a mere snack. I re-discovered this dish during my quest for one dish meals. Makes for a convenient lunch or dinner option as large quantities of bhaji can be made in advance and merely reheated before the meal. Served alongside perfectly toasted pao (buns), with oodles of butter.

Ingredients

45 mins   4 ppl

Onions: 2, finely chopped

Tomatoes: 3 finely chopped

Pao bhaji masala: 3 to 4 tbsps

Butter: 2 tbsps

Refined oil: 1 tsp

Lime juice: 2 tbsp

Pao (buns): 2 per person

Salt to taste

Mixed vegetables: About 500 grams, you can use beans, carrots, peas, potatoes, cauliflower

Method

1. Pressure cook the mixed vegetables with half a cup of water. Mash them well and keep aside.

2. Heat the oil in a wok, sauté the onions. Add the tomatoes and cook till soft. Add the mixed vegetables, pao bhaji masala and a cup of water. Simmer for 10 minutes. Add the butter and lime juice.

3. Served hot garnished with some fresh, finely chopped coriander

4. You can substitute the pao with multigrain bread or even regular roti. I love the 'chatpata' (translated that means sour and spicy) taste. Usually, I save some leftovers for my lunch box.

Note:
Pao bhaji masala is a spice blend and is readily available in any grocery store. You could alter the quantity of masala as per your family's taste. It may need you one or two attempts to get the spice levels right.

PANEER KEBABS
Grilled cottage cheese cubes with vegetables

When you think of cheese in the US, people come up with many different ones: Parmesan, Mozzarella, Blue Cheese, Cheddar etc. and Goat Cheese or Gorgonzola, if you are a connoisseur. For me, nothing beats fresh, homemade 'Paneer' or 'Chenna'. Technically, it is a type of cottage cheese, but the taste and texture is so refreshingly different. Making it is as simple as squeezing the juice of a lemon or two, into boiling milk. The paneer that you get by this process is usually mushy and dough like. This is the kind that I like to eat all by itself, with maybe a piece of fruit. This recipe however calls for paneer blocks, for which the home made paneer has to be squeezed till there is very little water left and flattened with some weights to get blocks of firm paneer. If you plan to make this dish, an easier way would be to buy it at the nearest Indian grocery store (usually available in the freezer section)

Traditionally, kebabs are meat based recipes. With the increase in vegetarianism and veganism, one has started seeing a plethora of experimentation with vegetable, soy and paneer based kebabs. Although it is not vegan, this vegetarian kebab is easy to make and an instant party favourite. Digging into these delicious, vegetarian kebabs makes me flirt with the idea of becoming a vegetarian for life. Seriously!

Ingredients

- Paneer (Cottage Cheese): 200 gms block
- Capsicum(Bell Pepper):1 Cup (medium size squares)
- Onion: 1 large (medium size chunks)
- Plain Curd (Yogurt): 2 tbsp
- Red Chili powder: ½ tsp
- Oil: 1 tbsp
- Haldi(Turmeric): A pinch
- Ginger Garlic paste: 1tbsp
- Garam Masala powder: 1 tsp
- Tandoori powder: 1 tbsp
- Salt: 1 tsp or to taste
- Dhania(Coriander): Finely chopped (for garnish
- Kali Mirch(Black pepper) powder: ¼ tsp)
- 10 wooden skewers

30 mins | 4-6 ppl

marination time
30 mins

Method

1. Cut the paneer into 2 inch cubes. Boil 2 cups of water and add a pinch of turmeric and salt to it. Remove from fire and add the paneer cubes to it. Let the paneer sit in it for about 5 minutes and strain the cubes. Immediately immerse in cold water. This ensures that the paneer has a nice yellow glaze on the outside and is soft on the inside.

2. In a large bowl, whisk the yogurt. Add the tandoori powder, garam masala, red chili powder, black pepper powder and salt. Marinate the paneer and the chopped vegetables (Onion and Bell peppers) in this mixture for about half an hour.

3. Skewer the vegetables and paneer, alternately. Make sure they are not too tightly packed. Do this in advance, but grill only when guests arrive to prevent the outer layer of paneer from hardening.

4. Spray some oil on an aluminium foil or a non-stick tray. Bake at 350ºC for 20 minutes.

5. Then broil on medium for 5 minutes so that the top layer becomes nicely browned

6. Garnish with dhania and serve immediately as an appetizer or a side. A dash of lemon adds a zest to this dish.

Note:
- Spraying with some butter or ghee (clarified butter) after the dish is done adds a nice flavour, moistness and glaze. If you are like me, and watching your fast expanding waistline, skip it.
- Using different colours of bell pepper makes the kebabs look even more appetizing
- Garnish with cilantro/coriander and serve immediately as an appetizer or a side. A dash of lemon adds a zest to this dish.

BAKED GOLD COIN PRAWNS
Yummy, baked appetizer

I grew up in a small town. For as long as I can remember, everyone knew everyone else. People from all states of India used to live there so it was quite a cosmopolitan environment. Those days, things were much simpler. You ate what you cooked at home. Restaurants in that small town simply did not exist. When I was in my teens, a new, swanky restaurant opened up on the beach. It was called 'The Golden Anchor'. This was something new for all of us. Even then, not everyone visited the restaurant. The main patrons of this restaurant were the business travellers and only a handful of us would visit with families on special occasions. The restaurant had a great chef and being a beach town, the place boasted of yummy, fresh lobster and seafood dishes. This is where I first tasted gold coin prawns. Over the years I have looked for this dish at restaurants but not many places serve this. When I moved to the US, I tried to experiment with a baked version with great results. So here it is-baked gold coin prawns.

Ingredients

30 mins   6 ppl

Large white bread: 8 slices
Eggs: 2
Onions: 1 medium finely chopped
Green chillies: 2, finely chopped
Water: 2 cups
Fresh ginger garlic paste: 2tbsps
Shrimps– 1cup (raw deveined, without head)

Dhania(Coriender): ½ cup, finely chopped
Til(Sesame seeds) – 2 tbsps
Salt: 1 tsp or to taste
Kali Mirch(pepper): ½ tsp
Butter: 2 tbsps

Method

1. Take a slice of bread and cut out 2 rounds out of it. (You can use a cookie cutter or a small bottle lid for doing this.)

2. Butter one side of the bread roundels and line on a cookie sheet, with the buttered side facing down.

3. Boil 2 cups of water and add the shrimps.

4. After 3 minutes, remove from fire and drain the shrimps.

5. Separate egg whites from the eggs and discard the yellow yolks.

6. In a blender, whisk the eggs, salt, chillies and ginger garlic paste for half a minute.

7. Add the shrimps and blend for half a minute. The mixture should be coarse and sticky.

8. Transfer to a bowl and mix in cilantro and black pepper.

9. Mix well and spoon this mixture on the bread roundels, patting it so that its sticks on the bread.

10. Sprinkle sesame seeds over the mixture and bake for 10 minutes at 250 degrees. Broil on low for the last 1 minute to get a golden colour on the top as well.

Note:
You can substitute boiled chicken or boiled crab meat to have a different variation of the 'gold coin'

SALAMI OLIVE ROLLS
A roll up appetizer

Starters actually set the tone for the meal that follows. Also as a large part of the evening is spent nibbling these starters they enjoy high share of mind space. It is easy to create fun and excitement with them and around them. Many have started to experiment with unusual ways to serve regular starters; definitely has a wow! effect.

With starters I feel you need to have a mix of some that can be served cold or quickly assembled. And some others that could be baked or fried or steamed or grilled and served hot. And of course assorted nuts and savoury mixes in small bowls lying within everybody's reach and getting refilled as necessary. I would especially for a smaller group throw in a big bowl of salad or stir fried veggies(depending on the weather) to serve as a substantial starter for those wanting to skip the main course; increasingly there are many who have started to do that.

Salami olive rolls is a really easy appetizer idea. Gets done in a jiffy and now I have trained my boys to make them. In fact it is so embarrassingly simple that I feel happier telling my guests that it's the kid's handiwork. With ingredients that are readily available at home this starter can be made a few hours ahead of the party and kept covered with a moist cloth to prevent the salami from drying up.

Ingredients

Salami roundels: 20

Green pitted olives: 20

Toothpicks- 20

Sandwich spread or mayonnaise or cream cheese: 2 tbsps. (optional)

10 mins   4 ppl

Method

1. Thaw the salami roundels- so take them out of the refrigerator at least an hour before you need to make them.

2. Once thawed spread them out on a plate or over a paper towel.

3. Spread some of the spread (if using) on the salami slices, place an olive over it and roll. Then let a toothpick run through it to hold them together.

4. If making without the sandwich spread then serve with a dip. Else just serve them on a platter with some olives alongside.

Note:
You could also halve the salami and olives and serve them like open boats with a toothpick in between holding it together. This also works well as DIY (do it yourself) starter where guests can decide if they want it with the spread or the olive or both. Kids are likely to say none and eat the salami just by itself.

Sometimes I serve the salami as roundels, with some tuna spread and topped with an olive. And any leftover gets used up in sandwiches the next day. I even cut the salami, olives and add them to my pasta.

HUMMUS
A delicious and versatile Middle Eastern chick pea dip

I find it amusing that my first taste of this Arabic/ Turkish dip was in the United States! A friend of mine with Lebanese-Greek lineage used to make it for almost all of her parties. Later I tried it at various restaurants and to my utter surprise, each time they would taste different. Almost like everyone had his or her own secret ingredient to make it special. Initially, I used to think that Hummus was some magical dip that would take hours to make. It was quite an anti-climax to eventually discover how simple it was to make. Even though there is a plethora of packaged Hummus available in the grocery stores, I still maintain that the freshest and the best Hummus that you can get is from your own kitchen!

Ingredients

Boiled Chickpeas (Garbanzo beans): 2 Cups
Tahini: 2 tbsp
Garlic: 3 large cloves
Olive Oil: 1 tbsp
Fresh Lemon Juice: 2 tbsp
Red Chilli Powder: ½ tsp
Salt:1 tsp
Dhania(Coriander)leaves finely chopped: 2 tbsp

 30 mins 10 ppl

Method

1. Place the beans, tahini, garlic, lemon juice, salt and paprika in a blender or food processor and blend till smooth.

2. Transfer to a serving bowl and drizzle Olive oil on top. Garnish with coriander and serve with pita chips/ warm soft pitas.

Note:
-Tahini (sesame seed paste) can be found in health food stores, gourmet shops and in many grocery stores.
-I use the fresh Garbanzo beans for this recipe. You have to soak it in water over night and boil it the next day till tender and then use it in the recipe.
-If you are using the canned beans, make sure you rinse it really well before you use it.
-This is the basic Hummus recipe. You can add olives or grilled red bell peppers while blending to add different flavours to your Hummus
-I usually serve it with pita chips or vegetable sticks like carrots, cucumbers etc. It can also be used as a healthy sandwich spread.
-Hummus tastes best when consumed fresh. You can also refrigerate it for about 7 -10 days without losing much flavour.

FETA AND WATERMELON STICKS
A fruity summer appetizer

I have already written about watermelon and how it revokes memories of Indian summers for me. This dish is a result of trying out new things from here and there and trying to provide lower calorie appetizers for my health conscious friends. I decided to experiment with cheese and watermelon with great results. This unusual fruity appetizer is very colourful in its presentation and satisfying. When you are serving other heavy appetizers like kebabs or chops or deep fried things, this serves as a good, fresh palate cleanser.

Ingredients

15 mins   **4 ppl**

Watermelon: 2 cups, cut into 1 inch cubes
Feta cheese: 3 tbsps
Pudina (Mint) leaves: 2 tbsps, julienned
Salt: ¼ tsp
Kali mirch (Pepper): 1 tsp
Lemon juice: 2 tbsps
Olive oil: 1 tsp
Honey: 1 tsp
Balsamic vinegar: 1 tsp (Optional)

Method

1. Take a big bowl and mix lemon juice, olive oil, honey and balsamic vinegar.
2. Arrange the watermelon on a decorative plate.
3. Drizzle the honey lemon dressing on top.
4. Sprinkle feta and mint leaves and serve.

Note:
You can add 1 tsp of sugar instead of honey for a different taste. You can also skewer watermelon and other fruits in a skewer for a fruit kebab effect.

CHUTNEY SANDWICH
A quick Indian sandwich

Sandwich is essentially not a traditional Indian concept. Bread used to be quite a foreign product; Indian breads are usually flat breads or rice cakes (idlis) which are very different from bread as understood by the western world. These days, bread is a staple breakfast item in India; as with both parents working it is difficult to rustle up traditional favourites like paranthas or upma for breakfast.

This dish is a little unusual as it combines cream cheese and traditional green chutney to create a spicy Indian spread. The tadka or tempering gives it an interesting spin and a crunch. It is a great appetizer that you can make a little ahead of time and garnish at the time of serving.

Ingredients

20 mins   **4 ppl**

Bread: 10 slices (white bread)

Cream cheese: 3 tbsps

Butter softened: 2 tsps

Pudina(Mint) chutney: 3 tbsps (1 inch ginger, 1 cup pudina, 1tsp salt and 2 green chillies ground to a fine paste)

For the tadka (tempering)

Mustard seeds: 2tsps

Curry leaves: 8-10

Ghee (Clarified butter): 1tsp

Method

1. Remove the brown edges of the bread and keep aside.

2. Mix chutney and cream cheese in a bowl and keep aside.

3. Spread butter on one side of all the bread slices.

4. Spread the chutney cream cheese mixture over the butter and make sandwiches (2 breads for each sandwich).

5. Cut each sandwich into 4 squares and place on a serving platter.

6. For the final garnish, heat the ghee in a small pan. Add the curry leaves and after a couple of seconds add the mustard seeds. When the seeds start to splutter, pour it on top of the bread and serve.

Note:
This dish tastes the best with plain white bread. You can try this with brown bread if you wish to.

BAKED CHEESY ONION DIP
A rich baked vegetarian dip to go with chips

Growing up in India, one grew up with the stereotype of all of western world loving meat and so logically, meeting a non-meat eating American was unthinkable. Although that description is probably true, living in the US for over 14 years now, I have had the opportunity to meet many vegetarians and vegans. The reasons are quite diverse. One elementary schooler gave up meat after she realized that she loves animals and that meat is obtained only after killing a living creature. A teen became vegan as she wanted to become a vet and really didn't fancy the idea of killing her future patients. And famously Bill Clinton became a vegan after having heart problems and realizing that the chief source of cholesterol comes from animal by-products. This dip I had in one of my vegan American friends that I later adapted to our tastes. Although this had cheese and is not truly vegan, it is a great accompaniment to chips or warm pita bread and is a great appetizer to serve.

Ingredients

30 mins   8 ppl

Sweet onions (red or white): 2 cups, sliced thin. (Use any white onion or red if you like)

Mayonnaise: 1 cup

Swiss cheese: 1 cup

Parmesan cheese: 1 cup

Salt: ¼ tsp

Kali mirch (Pepper): 1 tsp

Mustard seeds: 1 tsp

Curry leaves: About 12

Method

1. Take a big bowl and mix all ingredients.
2. Transfer to a baking dish and bake covered at 350 degree centigrade for 10 minutes.
3. Add the sugar and salt and remove from the fire.
4. Bake again without cover for 15 minutes
5. Serve hot with chips or pita bread.

Note:
This is a basic dip recipe. You can add sliced chillies, dhania (coriander) leaves or any other spice to add your own flavour. You can also experiment with different kinds of cheese, although cottage cheese or mozzarella will not work that well as they are not the melting type of cheese.

HUNG CURD DIPS
Low calorie, starter accompaniments

I dig starters and dips. There is something about those little nibbles, arranged daintily on toothpicks around the plate, picked up gently, twirled around in the dip and popped into the mouth; all the stages quite like a choreographed orchestra resulting in a gastronomical crescendo.

What is also amazing is that innumerable dips can be produced from some fairly basic and common place ingredients. My all-time favourite is using hung dahi (yogurt) as the base. I have tried several variations of it, mixed and matched the accompaniments. The result never fails to delight. I share below some of the dips that I have tried in the recent past.

Ingredients

hanging time: 2 hrs 10 mins 6-8 ppl

- Garlic: 2 tbsps finely chopped
- Green chillies: 2 tbsps, finely chopped
- Lime juice: 2 tbsps
- Pureed fruit or vegetable: 2 to 3 tbsps
- Mustard paste: 1 tbsp
- Salt: to taste
- Sugar: to taste
- Pepper: to taste
- Roasted jeera (Cumin): 1 tsp
- Pine nuts: 2 tbsps
- Pudina (Mint) leaves: 2 tbsps, finely chopped

Method

1. **Basic hung curd dip:** Add finely chopped garlic, finely chopped onions, finely chopped green chillies, sugar, salt, lime juice and pepper. This is typically served with cucumber with skin/carrots or with sautéed vegetables like mushroom, broccoli, carrots and beans.

2. **Strawberry dip:** Add pureed strawberry, black salt and a wee bit of sugar to hung curd, garnish with mint. Goes well with salted biscuits

3. **Palak (Spinach) dip:** Had this at a friend's place. Pureed and cooked spinach is added to hung curd. Add chat masala, bhuna jeera (roasted cumin) and salt to taste. She had served it with wafers (basic salted ones). Add some boiled American sweet corn, a dash of cheese and it would form a good canapé topping.

4. **Mustard dip:** Grind mustard, green chillies and a few pods of garlic to a fine paste. Add about a tablespoon of this to hung curd; add sugar (¼ tsp) and salt. I serve this with mustard potato (Marinate boiled potato with skin in a mustard curd marinade for a few hours. Sauté and serve along with the mustard dip). This dip would also go well as a topping for potato roundels, salted wafers, grilled prawns (lime juice, salt and pepper marinade).

5. **Mango dip:** I have made this with mayonnaise but I think it would do equally well with a hung curd base. Puree together two medium sized ripe mangoes, quarter cup of hung curd, quarter cup of chopped mint leaves, two tablespoons of pine nuts (expensive as an ingredient but adds body to the dip and loads of taste). Then add salt and pepper to taste. You could serve this either on krackjack/50-50(savoury-sweet) kind of biscuits or with cold cuts.

Note:
The best part about the dips is that you can serve them separately with the starters, use them as toppings, as fillings for salami/bread rolls, as sandwich spreads, even as a main course accompaniment with grilled chicken. So it is dip! dip! dip! all the way.

CURRY, DAAL & VEGETABLES

MOCHA GHANTO
Dry curry made of Banana flowers

With due respect to Charles Darwin, I have to confess that I do have the monkey genes! Just love bananas! In every form. In India, almost every part of the banana plant is consumed. The stem of the plant (thod or manja) is cooked with a mustard paste to make a delicious curry. My Mom boils it and adds it to plain yogurt to make a delightful raita. The raw green bananas become the raw materials for yum veg- etarian kebabs and curries. The yellow ripe ones, well those one you mostly eat as is, but it does show up from time to time in various Indian desserts. The leaves are usually used as disposable plates. Organic and green ...literally! There are also quite a few fish preparations where the fish is wrapped up in banana leaves and baked or steamed to gastronomic perfection. Let's now focus on the key ingredient of our recipe here The banana / plantain flower (mocha or bhanda as it is called in eastern parts of India). The banana flower is relatively easy to cook and delicious! The catch lies in cleaning and preparing the flowers for cooking. I will not lie. It is a tedious process. But it is not like you are going to cook it every day, so go for it. I can assure you, the re- sults are well worth it!

Ingredients

Banana flower: One medium inflorescence

Potato 1 large

Oil: 1 tbsp

Ginger (Fresh / Grated): 2tbsp

Jeera(Cumin seeds): 1 Tbsp

Fresh ground coconut : 2 Tsp Red Chili powder 1/2 tbsp

Roasted Jeera(Cumin seeds) powder: 1 tbsp

Salt: 1 tsp or to taste

Dhania(Coriander)leaves: 2tbsp finely chopped for garnish

Ghee(Clarified butter): 1tsp (optional)

60 mins **4-6 ppl**

Method

1. The banana flowers come packaged in a deep purple inflorescence. Yeah mother nature is quite the artisan. It has many florets neatly arrayed inside each leaf. Keep peeling the leaves and collect all the flowers in a bowl.

2. Take an individual flower; Open it up gently till you locate the stamen. It will be a black and relatively hard stem. Carefully remove the stamen and discard. Repeat for all the flowers.

3. Wash and clean the prepared flowers and soak for 15 minutes in a bowl of water to which a pinch of salt and turmeric has been added.

4. Drain the flowers and chop into small pieces. Peel and cut the potato into small pieces.

5. In a wok heat a teaspoon of oil. Add cumin seeds to it

6. When they start spluttering in 2 seconds or so, add the grated ginger.

7. Fry the ginger in oil for a couple of minutes. Add the potatoes and sauté for 4: 5 minutes.

8. Add the chopped banana flowers and sauté till the potatoes are almost done. Season with salt, chili powder and roasted cumin powder. Add grated coconut mix well. Remove from fire. Garnish with chopped dhania, ghee and serve hot.

DALMA
Yellow lentil cooked with vegetables

Dalma is a staple in Odia households. Roti and dalma is possibly the most common dinner menu you would come across. This is true across most regions of the state as well as across socio economic classes. Its strength and appeal lies in its simplicity. The kind of food that you reach out to, when you are looking for warmth and nourishment from within. Dishes that use a minimum of ingredients and spices, yet taste fabulous. One bite and you are filled with nostalgia. You immediately start to reminisce about mom/grand mom's cooking and happy, carefree times. Coming back in the good, old days to that familiar aroma and knowing in your heart that all was well. Easy to prepare, in three quick steps- boil daal, add vegetables (mix of green and starchy ones work best) and then the tempering. You are done. Retains an earthy flavour and tastes delicious.

Ingredients

45 mins

6 ppl

Arhar daal (Yellow Pigeon Peas): 1 cup

Haldi (Turmeric powder): ½ tsp

Ginger: ½ inch, pounded

Grated coconut: ½ tbsp

Jeera (Whole cumin): 1 tsp

Red chillies: 2 to 3

Potatoes: 2, quartered (large chunks)

Brinjal: 1 large, cut into large pieces

Parwal (Pointed Gourd): 3 to 4 halved

Arbi (Colocasia): 2, halved

Kaddu (Pumpkin): Half a slice (about 1/2 cup when cubed)

Sem (Broad beans): 2 to 3

Green banana: remove skin and chop

Roasted Jeera (cumin) and red chilli powder: 2 tsp

(Dry roast 2 tbsp of cumin and 3 to 4 red chillies separately and coarsely grind them together. Store in an airtight jar and use as required)

Mixed vegetables: Any four, all chopped the same size

Salt: to taste

Method

1. Pressure cook the daal with 3/4 cups of water, salt and turmeric. You must end up with a fairly runny consistency.

2. Transfer the cooked daal to a large kadai (wok). Bring the daal to boil. Add the ginger, vegetables - one by one starting with potatoes then followed by the others.

3. Cover and cook for a while, approximately 10 minutes, on low heat and then open and cook. There could be some scum on top, ladle it out.

4. Once the vegetables are done, separately prepare the tadka (tempering). Heat the ghee, add the whole cumin seeds. Once they sputter, add the red chillies and sauté for a minute or two. Add this to the daal vegetable mix.

5. Top with the grated coconut and the roasted cumin-chilli powder.

6. Serve hot with plain steamed rice or hot rotis.

7. Enjoy.

KASA TARKARI
Non spicy, mish-mash vegetable

Most of us, who cook, serve and eat non-vegetarian food struggle when it comes to serving an entirely vegetarian meal. No, don't get me wrong. I do cook and eat vegetables. In fact I can very proudly claim to eat them all- mother will vouch for this one. But it just seems way simpler to make a meal with a chicken curry or mustard fish thrown in. Given the inherent appeal of the core non-vegetarian ingredient you rarely go wrong. In whatever form you serve a non-vegetarian dish, people tend to relish it. Also, non-vegetarians treat the vegetarian accompaniments (what they call 'ghaas poos' meaning green, grassy stuff) as meant for lesser mortals and hardly pay any attention to them. So when you cook for a primarily non-vegetarian audience, you don't hone your vegetable cooking skills as much.

I find cooking with vegetables a lot tougher. Every element of the dish comes under much closer scrutiny. Overcooking the vegetable or overdoing the masala (spices) can completely ruin the dish. And getting the proportion and taste right requires great skill. When it comes to vegetarian exotica, I usually take refuge under eggless mayo, cheese sauces and butter gravies. Even tougher is making an interesting vegetable dish to go with home cooked Indian food. Over the years, I have finally mastered one called 'kasa tarkari' in Odia (loosely translated, it means stir fry). Though quite different from a stir fry in terms of both the process of cooking and the taste, it has a 'makha makha' consistency (neither dry nor watery gravy, somewhere in between). Traditionally eaten with puris and parathas but goes equally well with rotis.

Ingredients

- Potato: 2 large sized ones
- Tori (Ridge Gourd): 2
- Kaddu(Pumpkin): Quarter of a small pumpkin
- Parwal (Pointed Gourd): 4 or 5
- Brinjal: 4 or 5 small sized
- Onion: 1 (optional)
- Tomato: 1 large tomato
- Panch Phoran*: 1 tsp
- Oil: 1 tsp
- Dhania(Coriander) leaves: Finely chopped for the garnish
- Salt: to taste
- Haldi(Turmeric)- ½ tsp

45 mins 4 ppl

* Panch Phoran (meaning five spice blend) is a mixture of Methi (Fenugreek seeds), Kala Jeera (Black Cumin), Jeera (Cumin), Saunf (Fennel) and Ajwain (Carom seeds). Would be readily available as Panch Phoran in most Modern Trade stores .If not, add equal amounts of each ingredient to make 1 tsp.

Method

1. Cube all the vegetables. They should be the same size.
2. Heat the oil in a non-stick pan. Add the 'panch phoran' and let it sputter.
3. Next add the onions and sauté for a while till the onion looks glassy.
4. Add all the vegetables, salt, turmeric and cook on medium flame. Do NOT cover
5. Keep stirring the vegetables from time to time. The taste comes from this process of constantly moving the vegetables around (called 'kasiba' or 'ghantiba' in Odia).
6. The vegetables will release water and the dish gets cooked in the same. No need to add extra water. Cook till the vegetables are done.
7. The dish will have a mish-mashed look. Ridge gourd and pumpkin give it a natural sweetness.
8. Garnish with finely chopped coriander leaves and serve hot with rotis.

Note:
This dish uses very little oil, making it both healthy as well as flavoursome. One of my favourite accompaniments with paratha. Move over Alu Dam!

DAAL MAKHNI
Black lentil in creamy gravy

This dish is not for the fainted hearted, it is laden with butter and cream. And there is no leaner version. In most parts of the country, daal is considered a low involvement, low skill dish and often passed over for more interesting food . But in the North, and especially Punjab, it is main course, staple food. Chole kulche, rajma chawal, tandoori roti and daal makhni are popular combinations. Painstakingly cooked on slow fire, the daal is simmered for hours to bring out its real flavour.

This recipe has been sourced from a true blue Punjabi household. The instructions were very precise and easy to follow. The steps have also been simplified which makes it really easy for a first timer. I think the best tip I got was to use 'Roopak's' daal makhni masala. Thank God for blended masalas, easy to replicate the taste each time. And like one of the masala ad says, 'helps Mrs. Chawla make her sambhar as good as Mrs. Reddy's'. And in this case, a certain Misra master a complex Punjabi daal.

Ingredients

Saboot Urad Daal (Black Lentil): 1 cup
Rajma (Red Kidney beans): 1 handful
Tomato Puree: 10 to12 tbsps
Garam Masala: 1tsp
Cream: 1 cup
Daal Makhni Masala: 3 heaped tsps
Butter: 2 tbsps
Refined oil: 1 tsp
Garam Masala: 1 tsp
Water: 8 ½ cups

soaking time: overnight
60 mins
6-8 ppl

Method

1. Soak the daal overnight in 8 cups of water.

2. Pressure cook the daal with 8 cups of water and salt to taste (this daal cooks for much longer than regular daals, so do ensure you have added enough water else you risk burning it). Let the cooker give out one whistle and then cook on low flame for 40 minutes. Keep aside and let the cooker cool down naturally.

3. Take a kadai/wok and heat the oil. Next add the tomato puree and cook for 10 to15 minutes. Mix the daal makhni masala in about half a cup of water and add it to the tomato puree. Cook for another ten minutes. Add butter

4. Add the tomato puree mixture to the daal and let it simmer for 20 to 25 minutes.

5. Add the cream and 1 teaspoon of garam masala.

6. Served hot with rotis.

Note:
The kitchen smells lovely as the daal cooks. The daal has a smooth, creamy texture and all the ingredients blend beautifully together to create a rich, thick consistency. You will definitely have people asking for more. And for all you non-vegetarians reading this post, like I'd told my Dad years ago when I got home from the hostel, 'ghar ki daal, murgi barabar'.

BUTADALI ALU KAKHARU
Vegetable and lentil preparation

I stayed in hostels for over 7 years of my life and that makes me a non-fussy eater. In the first hostel where I spent nearly four years and made some friends for life, we were given only two meals a day (for the other two we had to fend for ourselves). And like Oliver Twist you could not ask for more. We did not want to anyway, the food was terrible. Our indulgent Moms would pack us tuck boxes which lasted us just about two days. Mine would also send me chowmein with loads of prawns every time my Dad was passing through the city. And we kinda survived. Food notwithstanding some of the happiest years of my life.

Though all dishes at the hostel without exception were bad, and we learnt to quietly eat them all; the dish that got discussed most often was the daal. It made an appearance at all meals. To the uninitiated, it took a while to figure out that the dish was actually daal. It was so watery in terms of consistency that it settled into two clear layers (remember your chemistry lesson on sedimentation; we got a live demo everyday), a ten inch watery one layer followed by a two inch daal layer. If you were the canteen didi's favourite she mixed up the daal and water layers swiftly before ladling it out onto your rice but if you had managed to rub her the wrong way all you ended with was a watery mess. When I went back home for the holidays, home cooked food, especially daal, took on an entirely new meaning.

Ingredients

30 mins   4 ppl

Jeera (Cumin) seeds: 3 tsp
Red chillies: 6
Haldi(Turmeric): ½ tsp
Salt: to taste
Dalchini(Cinnamon): 1 inch
Tej patta (Bay leaf): 1 or 2
Oil: 1 tbsp
Ghee (Clarified butter): 1 tsp

Chana (Bengal gram, skinned and split) daal: 2 cups
Kakharu (Pumpkin): 300 grams, chopped into large chunks
Potatoes: 200 grams, cubed, slightly smaller size than the pumpkin as the pumpkin will give out water and shrink during cooking
Ginger: 1 inch, chopped fine or grated

Method

1. Dry roast about 2 tsp of jeera with 4 red chillies and grind to a powder. Keep aside. This is the primary seasoning for the dish.

2. Soak chana daal for about an hour and then pressure cook with two cups of water for about 10 minutes (one whistle). Do not overcook the daal.

3. Next heat oil in a kadai/wok and add the bay leaves, 1 tsp jeera, 2 red chillies, grated ginger and sauté for a few minutes. Then add the potatoes and cook covered for about 5 minutes before adding the pumpkin. Add salt and turmeric. When the vegetables are almost done add the daal with the water, bring to a boil and then simmer for a few minutes. The daal should evenly coat the vegetables. There should not be too much gravy. Remove from fire and add the jeera- chilli masala.

4. Top with 1 teaspoon of ghee and serve hot.

Note:
Common breakfast item in Odia (Odisha is a state in the Eastern part of India) households and goes well with poori or luchis. Goes equally well with rice or rotis.

AVIAL
Mixed vegetable delicacy in a coconut and yogurt gravy

My family hails from the coastal region of Odisha, more specifically the district of Puri (one of the four holy places for Hindus). Dad loved to narrate the story about how his great grandpa traced our roots to Kannauj in Uttar Pradesh (Northern state in India). Our family had migrated to Odisha in 1230 AD. Someday soon, I hope to make my little pilgrimage to this town. For now, I am happy telling you my tales from the coast. As with any other coastal food, there is a fair amount of coconut in our cuisine. From our starters- nadiabada (coconut fritters) to desserts- pitha (dumplings stuffed with coconut and jaggery), we add them generously to our daals and curries, we even poach our fish and prawns in coconut milk to make some delicious, creamy stews. I think it is the absence of curry leaves and tamarind in our cooking that differentiates Odia coastal cooking from the others.

I also love sampling coconut based dishes from other regions of the country, be it coconut rice or chettinad chicken. Avial comes from Kerala, the southernmost tip of India. I like it for its minimal usage of oil and spices; the vegetables retain their taste and flavour. It is also very simple to prepare. Sampled several times in my Mallu (short for Malayalee, people from the state of Kerala) friend's lunchbox and then borrowed and recreated for my family.

Ingredients

60 mins   4-6 ppl

- Mixed vegetables (include vegetables like green banana, drumstick, yam, carrots, beans, snake gourd): 250 grams, cut into 1" pieces
- Haldi (Turmeric): ¼ tsp
- Grated coconut: 1 cup
- Jeera (Cumin): 1 tsp
- Green chill: ½
- Dahi (Yogurt): 1 cup, thick and well beaten
- Curry leaves: 6
- Coconut oil: 1 tbsp
- Salt to taste
- Water: 2 to 3 tbsps

Method

1. Grind the grated coconut, jeera and green chilli to a paste and keep aside.

2. Cook the vegetables with salt and turmeric (add just enough water to cook them, about 2 to 3 tablespoons).

3. Add the coconut paste to the vegetables, let it boil and then simmer for two minutes. Then add the dahi, mix well and remove from the stove.

4. Add curry leaves and coconut oil.

5. Serve hot

Note:
- You could skip the curd and add raw mangoes along with the vegetables.
- Locally grown vegetables like snake gourd or banana work best for avial. Modern day variations do use carrot and beans.
- While the recipe calls for using 250 grams of vegetables, one can use a little more or less of vegetables as one likes.

BAKED CABBAGE MANCHURIAN
A healthier version of Chinese staple

This post is dedicated to vegans. Due to health reasons, many of our family members and friends are turning vegetarian and even vegan and it is fascinating to see how they come up with healthier alternatives to traditional meat or fish dishes. Vegetable manchurian is a staple at most Chinese restaurants in India. They are typically made of seasoned carrots, cabbages and bell peppers shreds that are mixed with some ginger garlic paste, corn flour and deep-fried. These deep fried fritters are then tossed in a tomato garlic sauce and served hot with noodles. It tastes quite good but as you can imagine is loaded with calories, not to mention the fact that they are quite time consuming to make. This recipe is a much healthier baked version that is quick to make. Baking also ensures that it is a no fuss and minimal cleanup afterwards kind of recipe.

Ingredients

45 mins   6 ppl

- Cabbage – One small, cut into fine shreds about 2 cups
- Salt – 1 tsp or to taste
- Dhania (Coriander) leaves– 2 tbsps, finely chopped
- Ginger 1 inch+ Garlic 3 large cloves+ 1 green chili ground to a paste
- Carrots – One cup, finely shredded
- Dark soy sauce – 1 tbsp
- Tomato sauce – 1 tbsp
- Olive oil- 2 tbsps
- Onions- 1 cup, finely chopped
- Corn flour – 1 tbsp
- Kali mirch (Crushed pepper) – ¼ tsp

Method

1. Place the vegetables in a big bowl and lightly toss as you would for a salad.
2. In a small bowl, mix the soy sauce, ginger garlic chili paste and tomato sauce
3. Pour it on the vegetables and mix well.
4. Sprinkle the salt and pepper and toss for a couple of times.
5. Add the corn flour and mix well. The vegetables should be loosely sticking to each other. Add chopped dhania and drizzle the olive oil and mix.
6. Take a baking tray and line a nonstick aluminum foil.
7. Spoon the mixture in cookie sized dollops leaving a one inch space between each dollop.
8. Pre heat oven to 350 degrees and bake for 30 – 35 minutes.
9. Broil for the last 5 minutes to get a nice golden brown color. Serve hot.

Note:
You can substitute unflavored breadcrumbs instead of corn flour to get a crispy Manchurian. This dish needs to be served and eaten immediately. It becomes soggy if you leave it out and serve it later. Keep a close watch on the oven and adjust bake timings accordingly. If you don't want to bake, you can also shallow fry them in a table spoon of oil to get a "pakora" (fritter) version.

TANDOORI GOBHI
Whole baked, delicately spiced cauliflower

Every time I make this dish, I am reminded of my sister. She had just got married and was indulging in hectic entertaining that newlyweds typically do. And since the number of dishes she could make at that point of time hadn't even reached double digits, she would call me every time they had guests for dinner and ask me for recipes. I shared the recipe for tandoori gobhi (whole baked cauliflower), which she perfected. Only, she made that for every single dinner party for two consecutive years! It is a different story now that she has become a cooking expert, has her own food blog and is also co-authoring this book with me! A great menu addition for vegetarians and vegans, the baked whole cauliflower presents itself pretty well at the party circuits too.

Ingredients

Cauliflower: 1 Large
Sugar: 1 tbsp
Oil: 2 tbsps
Onions: 1 cup, finely chopped
Tandoori powder: 1 tbsp
Garam masala powder: 1 tsp

Tomatoes: 1 Cup, diced
Kali mirch (Black pepper): ¼ tsp, crushed
Salt: 1 tsp or to taste
Dhania (Coriander leaves): Finely chopped for garnish
Ginger: 1 inch + Garlic: 3 large Cloves, ground to a paste

6 hrs | 8-10 ppl

Garam masala can be prepared by grinding equal portions of dalchini(cinnamon), elaichi(cardamom), laung(clove) and kali mirch(whole pepper) to a fine powder. Proportion and ingredients could vary by region.

Method

1. Wash and clean the cauliflower nipping all the leaves and the hard stalks around it ensuring that just the full round head remains.

2. Take a large deep pan and heat a tablespoon of oil. Add sugar and heat till the sugar starts caramelizing and starts to turn golden brown. Reduce heat and immediately put the cauliflower head first into the pan. This is tricky. Watch the pan closely and make sure it doesn't burn. Lower the heat and after 1 minute add 1/4th cup of water and cover the pan.

3. Remove from fire after 5 minutes and keep aside. The cauliflower should be cooked al dente. Do not overcook.

4. In a separate pan, heat 1 tablespoon of oil. (I use olive oil but any vegetable oil will work)

5. Add the ginger garlic paste and fry till they are brown. Add the onions and cook till the onions look transparent. Add the diced tomatoes, tandoori masala and garam masala and 1/4th cup of water and cook till the mixture takes on a thick paste like consistency. Season with salt, remove from fire and allow the mixture to cool.

6. Smear the mixture all around the cauliflower. Put on a greased baking sheet and bake at 350 degree centigrade for half an hour. Garnish with chopped dhania and serve hot.

Note:
- Make sure the cauliflower is fresh and the florets are tightly stuck to each other.
- Tandoori masala powder and Garam masala powder are easily available in Indian stores.
- While smearing the masala make sure that you get some in between the florets and under the cauliflower.
- If you want to serve this as an appetizer, cut the cauliflower into small bite sized florets before baking and serve either with toothpicks or in pretty cupcake wrappers.
- You can put some fresh baby spinach around it while serving for decoration.

SANTULA
A light garlic flavoured vegetable stew

If you have had this dish or know how to make it, chances are that you are from Odisha or married to someone from Odisha (A state in India's eastern coast). Growing up, I have to admit that we were kind of forced into having this vegetable soup of sorts at regular intervals. Since, this dish is an Odia staple, if you were from Odisha, you ate santula. When I got married and set up my own home, I started experimenting with different cuisines. I have to admit that santula took a back seat; for a long time. Sometime back, we had a friend for dinner who wanted to eat something that was quintessentially Odia. I racked my brains for what to make and this was the only dish that I could think, which was as Odia as it gets. Absolutely unadulterated by influences from other states, this is what I cooked for her. In the process, I realized some other things, now that I was older and hopefully wiser. For instance, the vegetables and quick cooking process make it a dieter's and a nutritionist's delight. The dish is so mild in its flavouring, that it kind of refreshes your palate (like crackers during wine tastings) and actually makes you appreciate the other foods on your plate even more. Needless to say she loved it and santula was back on our family menu.

Ingredients

Pumpkin: 1 cup, peeled and cubed
Potato: 2 large, peeled and cubed
Baingan (Brinjal): 1 medium, cut into cubes
Zucchini: 1 medium, cut into cubes
Fresh green beans: 10 cut into 2 inch pieces
Carrots: ½ cup, cut into cubes
Tomato: 1 small
Salt: 1 tsp or to taste
Badi (Dried Lentil nuggets): 6

For the garnish (Tadka)
Mustard Seeds: 1 tbsp.
Jeera (Cumin) Seeds: 1 tbsp.
Green Chilli: 1 medium, cut into fine slices
Garlic: 4 large cloves cut into small slices
Dhania (Coriander) leaves: 2 tbsps, finely chopped
Ghee (Clarified Butter): 1tsp

 30 mins  6-8 ppl

Method

1. Take a tablespoon of olive oil and fry the badis till they are golden brown. Remove the badis onto a paper napkin to blot out the excess oil and keep aside.

2. In a separate container, take two and half cups of water and heat it for about 3 to 4 minutes.

3. Put the vegetables into the hot water in the order they cook, starting with the vegetable that takes the longest to cook. So in this recipe, starting with the potatoes, add pumpkin after 4 minutes, brinjal after 6 minutes. Cover the pan and when the potatoes are about 3/4th done, add cubed tomatoes and the beans. Cook for another 5 minutes. Just before removing from heat, add the badis. The dish is now ready for garnish or tadka.

4. Tadka is quite different from the regular garnishes. Also known as chaunk, baghaar or phoran, tadka is more of a tempering garnish and is typically used in Indian cooking as a finishing touch to dishes like daals, sambhaars or as in this case santulas.

5. Heat the ghee in a pan and add the mustard and jeera seeds.

6. Once they begin crackle and the mustard starts spluttering, Add chopped chilies and chopped garlic to the pan. Once the garlic is golden brown, pour the garnish on the santula, finish with fresh dhania and serve immediately.

Note:
- A lot of different vegetables can be used for this dish. My grandmother typically added okras and gourds. I am not particularly fond of those vegetables so I use beans and carrots instead.
- The vegetables in this dish are cut into largish cubes. Smaller may look better but will end up as a gooey mess and not form the stew texture that we are looking for.
- When you add more vegetables, make sure you add enough water to the pan when boiling.

STUFFED PARWAL
Masala filled pointed gourd

We all entertain from time to time, some of us more often than others. Many of us have the same guests coming over again and again, typically our closest friends/family. And while these are informal gatherings you still want to do something different, something exotic, to make your guests feel special. Selecting individual dishes to prepare is easy, but putting together an entire menu can be tough. Years ago, my sister had given me a very useful tip. She had said, "all your dishes need to look different". Even today, I use that as a basic filter when I am deciding on the recipes. Over the years, I have also made a few combinations that go well together and repeat the entire meal for different sets of guests with maybe a few minor tweaks here and there.

Parwal (pointed gourd) is a green vegetable indigenous to Eastern India. This stuffed parwal dish is my mother's recipe. I have never had parwal cooked this way in any other place. The story goes that we once had some unexpected guests and my mother did not have the time to make the regular stuffed parwal (where you painstakingly remove the seeds and stuff it with potatoes or masala or prawns or mince). So she did her own innovation and made an easier variation of the same. The guests loved it and since then it became a regular part of her entertainment menu. Off late, I have added it to mine. I call this dish Mama's parwal, as no other name captures its essence better. Mama is one of the most innovative cooks in the family. She has an excellent understanding of flavours and combines them with ease. Being a little restless by nature and always wanting to do something more, her recipes are quick and easy to replicate.

Ingredients

Parwal (Pointed gourd): 8 to 10 (about 2 per guest and a few extras)
Dhania(Coriander)powder: 1 tbsp
Jeera Powder (Cumin seeds powder): 1 tbsp
Chilli powder: 1 tsp
Salt: To taste, about 1 tsp
Haldi (Turmeric) powder: 1 tsp
Amchoor (Dry mango powder): 1 tsp (optional)
Oil: 1 tbsp

60 mins   **4 ppl**

Method

1. Place the parwal horizontally on the chopping board and make horizontal half slits along the length. Smear some salt and turmeric and let it stand for ten minutes. The vegetable will give out some water. Drain this out.

2. Next, mix all the masala together and stuff the parwal with the same.

3. Heat oil in a non-stick pan. Shallow fry the parwal, covering from time to time till done.

4. Serve hot.

Note:
It is a very quick way to transform an ordinary vegetable into something exotic. Goes equally well with a basic, everyday 'daal chawal' menu.

CHICKEN, FISH & MUTTON

BHANGA BESARA
Boneless fish in mustard gravy

It helps to have a set of interesting, easy to cook recipes in your everyday menu. Fish tops this list when it comes to non-vegetarian cooking. Given the increasing health awareness (no redmeat, no high cholesterol food), fish is gaining favour with an increasing number of people. For us Easterners, fish is usually part of our everyday food, quite like the daal chawal of our Northerner friends or the sambhar rice of the Southeners. My Mallu friend often jokes that Keralites also feel the same way about fish, so no meat days are literally so, 'no meat' but you can have all the fish you want to. My dad used to tell us that fish in the cities alongside the Ganges was referred to as 'Ganga kaphal' (fruit of the River Ganges), thus fit for consumption across castes (including the Brahmins) and communities.

Mustard fish is one of the more popular and well known fish dishes from the East. It requires very few spices and gets done in a jiffy. Bhanga Besara is a variation, a speciality of the region my family hails from. I have never eaten this dish in families outside of mine. So we have started to treat the dish as a 'family speciality'. Traditionally made with fish that was beginning to go a little bad (why else would you want to break the fish into smaller pieces), I tend to make it with boneless fish fillet which is a lot easier to cook and eat.

Ingredients

45 mins   4 ppl

Fish Fillet: ½ kilo

Potatoes: 4 medium sized

Panch phoran: 1 tsp

Haldi(Turmeric) powder: ½ tsp

Mustard oil: 1 tbsp

Ambula (Dried mango slices): 2

Salt: 1 tsp

Badi(Dried lentil dumplings): 6 to 8

Garlic flakes: 6 to 8

Green chillies: 3

Mustard: 2 tbsp

Choti Elaichi(Green cardamom): 2

*Panch phoran is jeera(cumin), saunf(fennel), kalonji(nigella), methi(fenugreek), sarson(mustard) seeds mixed in equal quantity.

Method

1. Smear salt and turmeric on the fish pieces and keep for about 10 to15 minutes.

2. Grind the mustard with 4 garlic flakes and one green chilli to a paste, keep aside.

3. Boil the potatoes and remove the skin. Dry roast the badi. Soak the ambula in water.

4. Heat the oil and once the oil begins to smoke, add the panch phoran, two green chillies and remaining garlic flakes. Saute. Next, add the fix and cook. Keep breaking the fillet as you fry the fish. This should take about 5 minutes.

5. Then, add one cup of water to the mustard paste and strain it, removing the black mustard skin. Add to the fish. Next, add the boiled potatoes- breaking them by hand as you do. Also add the soaked ambula and the dry roasted badi. Let them all simmer together for a couple of minutes. Then, add the green cardamom, adjust seasoning and remove from fire.

6. Serve with some plain rice, daal and a simple vegetable dish.

Note:
This preparation works well as part of a menu for entertaining; your guests however have to like fish in the first place.

FISH IN BANANA LEAVES
A flavourful and easy bake fish preparation.

One fish preparation that never fails to fascinate me is where the fish is wrapped in a leaf or foil of some kind and then steamed or baked. There are many reasons why I like this concept. One it is healthy as the recipe asks for baking or steaming which usually means no oil. Secondly, these kind of dishes are more flavourful as wrapping the fish seals in the flavours. Thirdly, it is hassle free and easy to prepare as no sautéing, frying or lengthy cooking process is involved. Last but not the least, pre made portion sizes and no mess clean up. Different provinces of India have different types of fishes baked in leaves. Western India has "patrani machhi" which is a Parsi speciality and Eastern India has "macher paturi" which is a Bengali speciality. This recipe is a fusion of the two. It is super simple to assemble and make. I like baking rather than steaming so that's what I have done in this dish. I have used pomfret (butter fish) for this dish. It works well with hilsa too.

Ingredients

marination time **15 mins**   **60 mins**   **4 ppl**

Pomfret fish: 2 large cut into 2 inch pieces (Total about 8 pieces- head discarded)
Coconut: ½ cup desiccated
Mustard seeds: 1tbsp
Ginger: 4 inches
Garlic: 8 cloves
Green chillies: 2 large
Dahi (Yogurt): 1 tbsp
Dhania (Coriander) leaves: ½ cup chopped
Oil: 1 tsp (Any oil will do; I usually use mustard)
Salt: 2 tsp
Fresh banana leaves: 8 large pieces

Method

1. Wash the fish and keep aside.
2. Grind the chillies, garlic, ginger, mustard seeds, dhania, yogurt and salt into a rough paste.
3. Add the fish and mix well until each fish is well coated. Let it marinate in this paste for 15 minutes.
4. Wash and trim the banana leaves.
5. Brush oil on to the glossy side of the banana leaf.
6. Place a fish on this making sure that you get enough of the coconut paste on both sides.
7. Carefully wrap up the banana leaf so as to make a square packet.
8. Finish up all the fishes in the same way. You should have 8 packets in all, one for each fish piece.
9. Heat the oven to 250 degrees.
10. On an ovenproof tray, line the fish banana packets in 2 rows making sure there is at least a 1 inch gap between the packets.
11. Bake in the oven for 40 minutes.

Note:
If you are out of leaves or find it difficult to get banana leaves, you can use aluminium foil instead. And if fish bones bother you, use boneless fillets instead.

BAKED FISH IN WHITE SAUCE
A light, creamy fish preparation

I have always been a little hesitant to experiment with fish. I usually cook it the traditional way. Rarely do I make fish when I am entertaining. If at all, then it is the good, old 'sorshe mach' (mustard fish) or a variation of it called 'bhanga besara' (makes an appearance earlier on in this book).

Also, people tend to be fussy about the kind of fish they eat. Many struggle with the bones and prefer to have it either fillet cut or made into chops and cutlets. I am also scared that the fish being so tender might break midway through the cooking, unless it has been fried as a first step in the process.

With experience and age, I have gotten brave and recently tried replicating my mother's baked fish. She uses a very quick and easy method to make the white sauce (if you can call it so). It also has no oil. Occasionally, when I am feeling a little indulgent, I add some grated cheese or a teaspoon of butter to enhance the flavour and taste.

Ingredients

baking time: 45 mins   15 mins   4 ppl

- Boneless fish fillet: 4
- Lime juice: 2 tbsps
- Salt: To taste
- Garlic cloves: 4 to 6, crushed
- Corn flour: 2 tbsps
- Milk: 2 cups
- Mixed herbs (like oregano, thyme etc.): 2 tsps
- Oil for frying the fish: 2 tbsps
- Butter: 1 tsp (optional)

Method

1. Marinate the fish in lime juice, salt and crushed garlic for 3 to 4 hours in the refrigerator.

2. Heat oil in a flat, shallow pan and sauté the fish turning it on both sides for them to brown. Once done place fish inside a baking dish.

3. Mix the corn flour with the milk. Add some salt, the herbs and whisk. Do ensure that there are no lumps. Transfer into a kadai (wok) and cook on high, stirring constantly. Remove from fire, add the butter, if using.

4. Pour over the fish to cover it completely.

5. Bake at 200 degrees centigrade for about 30 minutes, till the top starts to brown a bit.

6. Serve hot with some sautéed greens and buttered toast.

Note:
Rich, creamy taste with a hint of lemon and garlic; this dish is incredibly versatile and can easily be combined with a variety of options. Try serving it as part of a soup, sandwich and salad meal.

SWEET AND SOUR PRAWN
Chinese prawn accompaniment

If I had to name only one dish as my favourite, it would be my mother's 'sweet and sour prawn'. I view it as my mother's signature dish. No other dish comes anywhere close. Ever since I can remember, I have eaten it only out of my mother's kitchen. This is that one thing I have looked forward to eating each time I have visited my old home. It enjoys the same status as 'Motichur ladoo' (a type of sweet made famous by old Bollywood movies- epitome of mother's love) or 'Gajar ka halwa' (carrot pudding) for some others.

Sweet and sour prawn is undoubtedly, the most flavoursome dish that I have eaten and now, just about begun to cook. Mom was quite insistent that I try and make this dish at least once if I was planning to put it into the cookbook. It is a prawn based dish served in a chicken stock reduction. There is the tanginess of vinegar and tomato combine, the sweetness from the sugar and carrot, the crunch of the green vegetables, the full bodied chicken broth, delightfully tender prawns and the seasoning of pepper and soya. All the ingredients blend beautifully together to tantalize.

And while the list of ingredients and the stages seem a little complex to start with, once you have your head wrapped around this dish, and break the cooking into three stages, it is fairly easy. So get the wantons done, have the sauce mix ready and prepare the vegetables. Then, in less than ten minutes, you have a winner.

Ingredients

45 mins   **4 ppl**

- Prawn: 250 gms, medium sized
- Onion: 2, cut into rings
- Chicken stock: 2 cups
- Garlic: 3 flakes, crushed
- Tomato Puree: 1 cup
- Beans: 4, chopped
- Pepper: 1 tsp
- Carrot: 1, cut into thick roundels
- Vinegar: 1 tbsp
- Cabbage: ¼, cubed
- Sugar: 1 tbsp
- Capsicum: 1, cubed
- Corn flour: 4 to 5 tbsps
- Salt to taste
- Egg white: 1
- Soya sauce: 1 tbsp + 1 tsp
- Olive oil: 1 tbsp + Oil for frying

Method

1. Prepare the vegetables as detailed above. Parboil the beans and carrots.

2. Blanch the prawns in salt water. This is done by dropping the prawns into boiling water for about thirty seconds and then quickly immersing them in ice cold water. Drain.

3. Mix 2 tablespoons of corn flour with 1 teaspoon of soya sauce, salt and the egg white to form a batter. Dip the prawns into this batter and deep fry to make the prawn wantons.

4. Mix chicken stock, tomato puree, sugar, garlic, pepper, vinegar, 2 tablespoons corn flour and 1 tablespoon soya sauce to make the sauce mix. Keep aside.

5. Heat the oil in a kadhai/wok; add the onions and sauté for a few minutes. Next, add the capsicum, cabbage, beans and carrots. Add the sauce mix and when it comes to a boil add the prawn wantons. Simmer for a few minutes. Serve hot.

Note:
Goes well as an accompaniment with fried rice, boiled noodles or chowmein. I can have it just by itself at anytime of the day. For me, this dish is the taste of home- warm, inviting and nourishing. You could also boil the prawns in some salt water for a couple of minutes and add to the sauce instead of making the wantons. Do take care not to overcook the vegetables.

SORISA MACHA
Fish in mustard gravy

In the West, mustard is usually used as a sauce or paste to add flavour to salads, marinades and dressings. In India, many recipes use mustard paste to make thick curries. The taste is very sharp and blends well with meat and fish based dishes. As mustard is very overpowering in taste and smell, this is not really for everyone. However, if you are experimentative and would like to try something bold and flavourful, sorisa macha is for you. Sorisa macha (mustard fish) is a very popular dish in the eastern states of India- Odisha, Bihar and Bengal. Not sure where it originated from. During most of the British Raj, these three states were one single state and the division into Bengal, Bihar and Odisha came much later in 1911. Due to this, one finds a lot of overlapping culinary influences, although each state typically claims the dishes as their own. This is the Odia version of the dish.

Ingredients

40 mins | 4 ppl

Fish: 8 pieces, 2 inches thick
Mustard seeds: ¼ cup
Garlic: 8 cloves
Green chillies: 3 large
Oil: 2 tbsps for frying and 1 tsp for garnish
Grated coconut: 1 tbsp
Salt: 2 tsps
Haldi (Turmeric): 1 tsp

Kalonji (Onion seeds): 1 tsp
Jeera (Cumin) seeds: 1 tsp
Dhania (Coriander) leaves: A few stems chopped fine for garnish
Water: 1 cup

Method

1. Soak mustard seeds in 2 tablespoons of water and keep aside for 15 minutes.
2. While the mustard is soaking, wash the fish and pat dry.
3. Add 1 teaspoon turmeric and 1 teaspoon of salt to the fish and mix well.
4. Shallow fry in oil till half done and keep aside.
5. In a blender, grind the soaked mustard seeds, 2 chillies, garlic and coconut into a fine paste.
6. In a pan, heat 1 teaspoon of oil and put the onion seeds and the cumin seeds along with the remaining green chilli split into half.
7. After about 15 seconds, when the cumin seeds turn brown, add the fish and sauté for a minute.
8. Add the mustard paste and one cup of warm water.
9. Reduce heat, cover and simmer for about 10 minutes till the fish is done.
10. Garnish with the coriander leaves and serve hot.

Note:
Ideally, rohu fish (carp) works best for this dish. Although you can use any kind of oil, mustard oil gives it its distinctive flavour. I sometimes add 1 tablespoon of yogurt to the mustard paste while grinding, for a slightly different tart flavour. Some people also drizzle a bit of mustard oil as a garnish, right before serving.

DAHI MAACHA
A traditional East Indian fish in yogurt gravy

Yogurt fish or dahi maacha as it is called in Odia is a typical, East Indian preparation. If you google this dish you will find plenty of recipes, each very different from the other. I may be a little biased, but the best dahi maacha I have ever had is the one my Mom makes. I have never bothered to write down the recipe as I always call my Mom when I want to make this dish. Today was no different. I just got off the phone talking to her and getting all the details about this recipe. Even though she had just gotten up, was still groggy and drinking her morning tea, she patiently listed out the exact measures and the procedure to me, like only a mother would. At least now I have this recipe in print and don't have to call her at unearthly hours (due to the time difference), every time I feel the urge to make this dish.

The thing about yogurt is that it tends to curdle at high heat, so this recipe calls for simmering semi cooked fish on low heat. The addition of a little bit of sugar in the yogurt mixture also helps. When in India, I use rohu fish for this recipe. In the US, I use carp.

Ingredients

marination time: 15 mins 20 mins 6 ppl

- Fish: 12 pieces, 2 inch size
- Dahi (Yogurt): 1 ½ cups
- Onion: 1 medium sized, finely diced
- Green chilies: 2, slit into 2 pieces
- Ginger: 2 inches chopped
- Garlic: 3 large cloves, chopped
- Sugar: 1 tsp
- Oil: 2 tbsps
- Salt: to taste
- Haldi (Turmeric): 1 tsp
- Kali mirch (Black pepper) ground: 1 tsp
- Elaichi (Cardamom): 4
- Dalchini (Cinnamon) sticks: 2
- Laung (Cloves): 4
- Saunf (Fennel): 2 tsps
- Water: ½ cup

Method

1. Wash the fish pieces; add salt and turmeric.

2. In a non-stick pan, heat 1 tablespoon oil and fry the fish till half done (about 5 minutes).

3. Keep aside till it cools down to room temperature (about 10 minutes).

4. Mix the dahi with sugar, salt and pepper powder. Marinate the fish pieces in it once they have cooled down. Let it stand for about 30 minutes. It is essential that the fish is cool and not hot when you add it to the yogurt mixture.

5. Grind the green chillies, garlic and ginger with about 1 tablespoon of water to a fine paste.

6. In a pan, heat the remaining oil. Add the saunf, dalchini, laung and elaichi. Add the chopped onions and fry till the onions are glassy. Then add the ginger, garlic, green chilli paste and sauté for 10 minutes.

7. Reduce heat and add the fish yogurt mixture.

8. Simmer on low heat till the fish is cooked through. This should take about 10 minutes.

9. Serve immediately with hot rice.

Note:
You can also try this recipe with Jumbo shrimps. Delicious.

MACHA HALDI PANI
Traditional Odia fish stew

Food, they say, is the most primitive form of comfort. Every family has their own comfort food recipes, like moong daal khichdi with achar; rice, daal and mashed potatoes; bread with chicken stew; konji etc. The common theme across these seemingly varied dishes is that they are home-made, warm, filling, unpretentious and provide easy satisfaction. Most of them use very few ingredients, are quick to prepare and help you reach an improved emotional status almost instantly. Just what the doctor ordered, on a day you feel low, stressed, home-sick or nostalgic. Growing up in a small, though cosmopolitan town, my early food memories (apart from the dishes at home) are of those that got cooked in our neighbours' kitchens. So it was Kumar aunty's rajma, Murthys aunty's idlis, Smith aunty's vindaloo, Padmanabhan aunty's sambhar, Nanda aunty's cakes, Mohanty aunty's malpuas.....I could go on and on. Food, that brings back comforting, childhood memories. Although far from gourmet, it invokes a feeling of nostalgia and security. It also makes for good food stories and helps us children connect, even years later. Incidentally, mom managed to learn almost all of these dishes and soon they got cooked in our kitchen too. But, they were always referred to by the names of their original creators/disseminators. In the pre-cookbook/pre-cookery show days, recipes travelled through word of mouth and personal demos. There was a lot more active sharing and sampling. We eagerly looked forward to what our neighbours were going to send us next.

Macha Haldi Pani is a commonly cooked, fish dish in any Eastern household. The recipe could vary slightly from family to family. Like, some I know would skip the ginger, others might replace tomatoes with dried mango (ambula), and some others might make it sans the vegetables. But whichever way you cook, it sure comforts.

Ingredients

45 mins   4 ppl

- Rohu Fish: ½ kilo
- Potatoes: 2 to 3, cubed
- Cauliflower: 8 to10 florets
- Tomatoes: 2 finely chopped
- Ginger: ½ inch, finely grated
- Chilli powder: ½ tsp
- Haldi(Turmeric) powder: ½ tsp
- Dhania (Coriander)powder: ½ tsp
- Whole Jeera(Cumin): 1 tsp
- Jeera(Cumin) powder: 1 ½ tsp
- Mustard Oil: 2 to3 tbsps
- Garam Masala: 1 tsp
- Tej Patta (Bay leaves): 2
- Water: 2 ½ cups

Method

1. Smear salt and turmeric on the fish pieces and keep for about 10 to15 minutes.

2. Heat the oil and once the oil begins to smoke, add the fish and shallow fry for a few minutes. Remove and keep aside. The fish should be a little soft.

3. Into the same pan, add some whole jeera and the bay leaves. Once the jeera begins to sputter, add the cubed potato and cauliflower florets and fry for a couple of minutes. Mix the dhania powder, jeera powder, turmeric powder, chilli powder, grated ginger in about half a cup of hot water. Add it to the potato and cauliflower. Add the tomatoes.

4. Saute for a few minutes, till the masala coats the vegetables. Add two more cups of hot water to the dish and allow the gravy to come to a boil. Check salt and other seasoning.

5. Add the fish pieces and let them simmer. Finally add the garam masala.

Note:
Goes best with some plain rice. The vegetables, together with the fish, make it wholesome and balanced.

ALLEPEY FISH CURRY
A spicy and tangy fish curry in coconut gravy

Being from the East one is typically used to cooking the fish in mustard oil. Preparations range from 'jhola' which is light thin gravy to 'sorisa' or mustard fish or 'dahi macha', a curd based fish curry. There are a couple of variations in between and then there is the fish head which is cooked with vegetables or pulses.

This recipe comes from down South and from a very authentic source. My friend insists that I call it Allepey fish curry and not Kerala fish curry. There are subtler and finer differences in ingredients, flavoring and the method of cooking. She is a very good cook herself and transforms mundane everyday food into finger licking delicacies. So I shall go by what she says.

Ingredients

 20 mins   4 ppl

- Fish (Rohu/Seer): 6 to 8 pieces
- Kashmiri red chilli powder: 2 tsps
- Haldi (Turmeric) powder: ½ tsp
- Thin coconut milk: 1 ½ cups
- Thick coconut milk: ½ cup
- Coconut oil: 1 tbsp (could substitute with any other refined oil)
- Curry leaves: 20
- Salt to taste
- Methi (Fenugreek) seeds: 1 tsp
- Small sambhar onions (Shallots): 5/6
- Ginger: 1 inch
- Green chillies: 1/2
- Kacha aam (Green mango): 1, remove skin and cube

Method

1. Pound the onion, ginger and green chillies together, keep aside.
2. Heat oil in a flat pan and fry the methi seeds for a minute or two.
3. Add the onion, ginger, chilli mixture and sauté for a few minutes. Add the curry leaves.
4. Then add the thin coconut milk, mango pieces, salt, chilli powder and turmeric, mix well.
5. Drop the fish pieces into the gravy. Let it come to a boil then cover and cook.
6. After 10/15 minutes or once the fish is done, open the lid.
7. Add the thick coconut milk, few curry leaves.
8. Finally could add a teaspoon of coconut oil on top

Note:
Has a very distinct and lingering flavour. The tartness of the mangoes beautifully balanced by the sweet, creamy coconut milk.

PRAWN CURRY
Succulent prawns in a light masala gravy

Unless you are allergic to prawns, you are sure to love them. Whether boiled, sautéed, grilled, baked, fried, stewed, curried this versatile fish (technically crustacean) tastes good in all forms. The only tip to remember is to never overcook them. Then they get all hard, dry and rubbery. So just toss them in, wait for the colour to change and out they go. If adding straight into the gravy, bring them in during the final stages of cooking. Some recipes call for pawns to be cooked with their shell. While this gets a little messy to eat, once you have managed to get beyond the top layer, there is delightfully flavoursome, soft flesh beneath.

Being from the coast, prawns were quite popular in our household and cooked with regular frequency. Mom tried several versions too-chilly prawns, stir fry prawns with some soya, vinegar, bell pepper, chillies, onion, garlic and tomatoes to a succulent finish. Yummy! And then of course, prawns in a mustard base, prawns in a coconut gravy etc. Actually prawns lend themselves quite easily to all kinds of cuisine- toss a handful into pasta, fry them with some butter and pepper, cook them with some rice and veggies for a most delicious pulao, add them to your salads for flavour, body and taste.

This curry is a more basic version. Quite easy to prepare, just stir together a few basic ingredients and you are done. Delicious.

Ingredients

45 mins   **4 ppl**

- Prawn: 250 gms, medium sized
- Onion: 2, finely chopped
- Garlic: 4 to 5 pods, finely chopped
- Ginger: 1 inch, grated
- Choti Elaichi(Green cardamom): 3
- Dalchini(Cinnamon): 2 inch sticks
- Tej Patta (Bay leaves): 2
- Jeera (Cumin seeds): 1 tsp
- Tomato: 2, finely chopped
- Potato: 2, cubed
- Ghee: 1 tsp
- Mustard oil: 2/3 tbsp.
- Jeera (Cumin)powder: 1.5 tsp
- Dhania (Coriander)powder: 1 tsp
- Chilli powder: 1 tsp
- Haldi(Turmeric) powder: 1 tsp
- Green chillies: 2
- Salt to taste

Method

1. Heat the oil in a wok/kadai till it starts to smoke.

2. Add the prawns (to which ½ teaspoon turmeric powder and ½ teaspoon salt has been added), sauté for a few minutes only. Remove.

3. Into the same wok, add the cumin seeds, bay leaves, onion, garlic and fry for a couple of minutes. Add the cardamom and cinnamon sticks. Next, add the cubed potatoes, salt and once the potatoes have cooked sufficiently, mix the grated ginger and dry spices (cumin, coriander, turmeric and chilli powder) with a little bit of water and add.

4. Toss the masala around to evenly coat the potatoes. Then, add the tomatoes and cook till the tomatoes soften.

5. Add a cup or two of hot water and let the gravy come to a boil. Toss in the prawn and let them cook for about 5 to 7 minutes. Garnish with slit green chillies. Check the salt and add more if necessary.

6. Finish off with some ghee. Serve hot with plain steamed rice.

Note:
A very simple meal that leaves you feeling satiated- that, I think is the power of simplicity.

DAAB CHINGRI
Shrimps in a creamy mustard sauce baked inside a tender coconut shell

In India you find a lot of permutation and combination of recipes with seafood and coconut especially in the coastal belt. I ate "Daab Chingri" (Green coconut shrimps) for the first time in Calcutta (now known as Kolkata). The combination of mustard paste and shrimps slow roasted in a green coconut shell was really something out of this world! And the fact that it is served straight from the oven to the table in the same coconut shell makes of the wow factor. The nice thing about this recipe is that the ingredients are not that many and the process is rather easy. The shrimp kind of melts in your mouth and the dish is light and creamy at the same time. Rotis or Rice are great accompaniments.

Ingredients

15 mins 4 ppl

Whole Green Coconut: 1

Shrimps Small or medium sized: 1 Cup

Mustard seeds: 3 tbsps

Garlic: 2 large cloves

Haldi(Turmeric) Powder: 1/4 Tsp

Green chilies: 2 cut into thin slices

Dhania(Coriander) leaves :1/2 Cup finely chopped

Salt to taste

Red Onion:1 medium cut into very small cubes

Fresh grated coconut: 2 Tbsp

Preparing the Coconut

Tender coconut or green coconut is easily found in the Indian or Interna- tional stores. Make sure that it is cut in such a way that there is a base for it to sit. Slice off the top of the coconut and drain out the coconut water. (Co- conut water makes for a delicious drink by itself) The hollow of the coconut along with the tender coconut inside is where we will stuff the shrimps.

Method

1. Make sure the shrimps have been cleaned and deveined

2. Blend the mustard seeds, green chilies and garlic till they become a fine paste.

3. Mix all the ingredients with a spatula except the besan.

4. In a bowl mix the shrimps with the paste. Add the chopped on- ions, grated coconut, turmeric, salt and cilantro. Mix well.

5. Take the coconut shell and use a small spoon to carefully spoon in the shrimp mixture into the shell, Do not over stuff the shell.

6. After some time (about 20 25 minutes) you will notice that the mixture begins to take on dough like consistency and starts to move together like a ball.

7. Take the top of the shell that you kept aside while draining the water out and press onto the stuffed shell so that it appears to be a whole coconut and forms an air tight "container" for the fish to bake in.

Note:
-Preheat the oven to 400 degrees. Place the stuffed coconut in the oven and bake for an hour. Remove from the oven when done and serve immediately.
-top. You can get the grocery shop to do this for you. Just make sure you use the coconut the very same day as it is cut.
-Fish dishes are tricky when it comes to salt. Less is really more :)

GHEE ROAST CHICKEN
The famous chicken side dish from Mangalore

I approached this dish with some trepidation. To start with ghee, roast and chicken are not foods that go together in my head. Ghee is usually not the enabler when it comes to non-vegetarian food and I prefer good old mustard oil for almost all my fish and meat dishes. Next, 'roasting' is a term I associate with western cooking; I do make a whole roast stuffed chicken and variations thereof but in the oven, seasoned with herbs and sauces and the skin left on. The recipe also calls for three souring agents (yogurt, lime juice and tamarind) and that had me a little worried initially. But the spices and the jaggery balance out the sourness beautifully. In fact this dish is all about balance and not overdoing any part of it. A fairly elaborate recipe with a long list of ingredients, but well worth your time. Somebody described the dish as a "culinary gem" and that is no exaggeration. Also you could do some of the prep work in stages. Like, marinate the chicken from the night before (though the recipe calls for two hours, the longer the better), grind the masala paste and refrigerate as roasting the masalas takes up bulk of the active cooking time. And you need to be patient through the stages. The end result being delightfully succulent, spicy chicken with a hint of sourness and the unmistakeable flavour of ghee.

Ingredients

60 mins **4-6 ppl**

- Chicken: 1 kilo
- Lime juice: 1 tbsp.
- Dahi (Yogurt): 4 tbsps.
- Haldi (Turmeric): 1/4th tsp.
- Red Chillies: 10, soaked and de-seeded
- Garlic: 1 whole (20 pods), chopped
- Dhania (Coriander) seeds: 2 tbsps.
- Jeera (Cumin): 2 tsps.
- Kali mirch (Black pepper): 1 tsp.
- Cloves: 3
- Methi (Fenugreek) seeds: ½ tsp.
- Tamarind: Lime sized ball (deseeded)
- Ghee (Clarified butter): 5 tbsps.
- Gud (Jaggery): 1 tsp., grated
- Curry leaves: 15/20
- Salt to taste

Method

1. Whisk together the yogurt, lime juice, salt and turmeric. Marinate the chicken pieces in it for about one or two hours.

2. Soak the tamarind in some lukewarm water for about 15/20 minutes.

3. Dry roast the red chillies and remove. Then in about 2 teaspoons of ghee roast the dhania, jeera, clove, methi and kali mirch. Grind to a fine paste together with the tamarind and garlic. Keep aside.

4. Heat the rest of the ghee in a kadai/wok and fry the chicken pieces in it. Cook on high flame for the first five minutes and then covered on low flame till the chicken is almost done. Remove the pieces onto a plate, let the marinade remain in the kadai.

5. Add the ground masala paste to the marinade and cook for about 10 minutes on high flame, stirring constantly. The masala should have turned dark brown.

6. Add the chicken pieces back and mix well so that the masala coats the chicken evenly.

7. Add the jaggery and finally the curry leaves. One final stir and you are done.

8. Serve hot with rice or roti.

9. After 5 minutes, add 1 cup of water and bring the mixture to a boil.

Note:
Please don't wince at the ghee; as the name suggests it is the key ingredient in this dish. Helps keep the chicken moist, juicy and tender. Leaner versions don't work, trust me.

CHICKEN KHUS KHUS
A rich, flavourful chicken curry with khus khus (poppy seeds)

I am not really sure where this recipe came from. Possibly was a result of trial and error on my part. When you watch amazing cooks like my mother or grandmother cook, you can be sure of picking up some nifty tricks on the way. Adding cashew paste or khus khus (poppy seeds) paste or coconut juice to thicken gravies, for instance. Sprinkling a little water on stir fries to help them cook while retaining their crunch is another. And so on. I guess, somewhere along the way, I began to add to add poppy seed and cashew paste to my regular chicken curry recipe as they taste better and not because I messed up the gravy. Anyway here it is …

Ingredients

45 mins   6 ppl

- Chicken: 2 cups, cut into small cubes
- Onion: 1 medium size, diced into tiny pieces
- Green Chilies: 2 cut into small pieces
- Curd(Yogurt): ¼ cup
- Ginger: 2 inches chopped
- Dhania (Coriander) leaves: 1 small bunch, chopped fine
- Garlic: 3 large cloves, chopped
- Cashew: 2 tbsps
- Coconut milk: ¼ cup
- Sugar: 1 tsp
- Oil: 1tbsp
- Poppy seeds (Khus Khus): 2 tbsps
- Salt: to taste (about ½ tsp)
- Kali Mirch(Black pepper) ground: 1 tsp
- Garam masala powder: 1 tsp
- Water for cooking: 1 cup

Method

1. Soak the poppy seeds and cashews in half a cup of warm water. After 10 minutes, grind with a little water to a fine paste and keep aside.
2. Grind the green chillies, garlic and ginger to a fine paste and keep aside.
3. Beat the yogurt with ½ tsp salt and pepper. Marinate the chicken in it for at least 30 minutes.
4. In a pan, heat the oil and add the sugar.
5. As soon as the sugar starts becoming light brown, add the onions and stir lightly.
6. Add the chilli ginger garlic paste and fry for 5 minutes.
7. Add the marinated chicken pieces.
8. Stir from time to time, till the chicken is semi cooked.
9. Add the poppy seeds and cashew paste. Stir till it is well mixed and cover the container.
10. After 5 minutes, add 1 cup of water and bring the mixture to a boil.
11. Reduce heat and add the coconut milk. Cook till the chicken is cooked through and the gravy is thick.
12. Garnish with garam masala powder and dhania. Serve hot.

Note:
This recipe tastes great with roti or rice. Thicken the sauce a bit if you want to have it with rotis and make a thin sauce by adding 1/4th cup extra water when you want to have it with rice.

MEXICAN CHICKEN
Basic grilled chicken

After cooking for over two decades, most recipes tend to have a familiar ring to them; a feeling of 'been there done that'. For instance, Indian chicken curries are likely to be dahi (yoghurt) based or tomato based, pastas are cooked primarily in white sauce, a tomato base, or just tossed around in olive oil, basic daals would either have a jeera (cumin) or rai (mustard) tempering and so it goes.

Yet, the mere addition of even one new ingredient or varying the proportion of a familiar ingredient or adding it during a different stage in the cooking, changes the complexion of the dish entirely. This fact gets reinforced each time I make an Indian chicken curry. Using almost the same ingredients- tomato, onion, ginger, garlic, coriander powder, jeera (cumin) powder, I get a very different end result each time. Dhania (coriander) chicken, elaichi (cardamom) murg have different tastes. Even with the dahi (yoghurt) based chicken dishes whether you marinate the chicken in the dahi or add whipped dahi towards the last stages of cooking impacts the texture, consistency and taste. Ditto for coriander leaves, which when added towards the end as the garnish enhances the sensorial but when added earlier on adds to the taste and richness of the gravy.

Mexican chicken however uses an entirely different set of ingredients. Orange juice gives it a mildly sweet flavour which gets balanced by the sour lime juice. The overnight marination also ensures that the chicken is wonderfully seasoned and oozing with taste.

Ingredients

45 mins 2 ppl

Chicken: 500 gms

Garlic: 5 cloves, chopped fine

Orange juice: ½ cup

Lime juice: 4 tbsps

Chilli sauce: 1 tsp

Dhania (Coriander) leaves: 2 tbsps

Kali mirch(Pepper): 1 tsp, freshly ground

Corn flour: 2 tsps

Salt: to taste

Method

1. Combine the orange juice, lime juice, garlic, chilli sauce and the coriander leaves. Use this as a marinade for the chicken. Let the chicken marinate in the refrigerator for 8 hours or overnight.

2. Heat a non- stick pan and cook the chicken in it for about 20 minutes, till it turns to brown on both sides. Add the pepper powder. Remove the chicken pieces once done onto a plate.

3. Mix the corn flour with the remaining marinade in the pan and let the sauce thicken a bit. Pour over the chicken.

4. Serve together with some sautéed buttered greens and mashed potatoes

Note:
Also, combines beautifully with spaghetti. Use the leftover chicken in salads or spice it up with some chilli flakes and onions to make the filling for a wrap. Though, going by my experience, you are unlikely to have any leftovers.

BUTTER CHICKEN
Succulent chicken in a creamy tomato gravy

Any dish that is cooked in butter and laced with cream is most likely to come from Punjab (Northern part of India). The Punjabis are unmatched in their zest for life and this is reflected in their cuisine. Wholesome and filled with full bodied flavour of spices. Usually cooked in desi ghee (clarified butter) and served with dollops of butter or cream. As with Punjabi large heartedness there is a feeling of abundance around these dishes. And when talking about Punjabi food, butter chicken tops the charts. Definitely not a dish for the calorie watchers or faint hearted, but hard to resist, nevertheless.

The chicken pieces are absolutely succulent and the creamy gravy has a sweet-sourish taste. Undoubtedly, one of the most popular dishes from India, it is quite easy to prepare this delicious, melt in the mouth treat. Ready to use, blended spice mixes have made it even easier.

Ingredients

marination time		
4-5hrs	60 mins	4-6 ppl

For the tikka
- Choti elaichi (Green cardamom): 2
- Dahi (Yogurt): 4 tbsps
- Kashmiri red chilli paste: 1 tsp
- Ginger garlic paste: 1 tbsp
- Garam masala*: 1 tsp
- Sugar: 1 tsp
- Butter (for frying): 1 tbsp
- Oil: 1 tbsp
- Chicken: 1 kilo, boneless cubed

For the gravy
- Tomato puree: 2 cups
- Cream: ½ cup
- Butter: 1 tbsp
- Salt: 1 tsp or to taste
- Kashmiri red chilli powder: 1 tsp
- Kasoori methi (Dry roasted fenugreek leaves): 1 tsp
- Javitri (Mace): 1 gm
- Salt: 1 tsp

*Garam masala is a blended spice prepared by grinding together laung (cloves), dalchini (cinnamon), tej patta (bay leaf), jaiphal (nutmeg), javitri (mace) and kali mirch (black pepper). The composition differs as per personal and regional tastes. Ready to use packaged versions are readily available.

Method

1. Whisk the dahi, one tablespoon of oil, one tablespoon of ginger garlic paste, red chilli paste, garam masala and about one teaspoon of salt together. Marinate the chicken pieces in it and leave them to refrigerate for 4 to 5 hours.

2. Heat one tablespoon of butter in a flat pan and fry the marinated chicken pieces in it. Let them brown. Then remove and keep aside.

3. To make the gravy, heat one tablespoon of butter in a kadai (wok). Add the green cardamom and mace, cook till fragrant. Next the ginger garlic paste and sauté for about 5 minutes. Then add the tomato puree, chilli powder, salt and sugar. Mix well and simmer for 10 to 15 minutes, till the puree is completely cooked. Finally, add the kasoori methi.

4. Drop the chicken tikka pieces into the gravy and continue to simmer for another ten minutes.

5. Fold in the cream and remove from fire.

6. Serve hot with some roti or naan.

Note:
- Butter chicken and chicken tikka masala are available in all grocery stores across the country.
- You could also use store bought chicken tikkas for this recipe; follow the method for the gravy and drop the tikkas into it.

COOKING UP A STORM - *THE MISRA FAMILY WAY*

KHOW SUEY
Burmese chicken curry with noodles

Khow suey is definitely my favourite one pot meals. Even the name and especially the way you roll your tongue as you say the word has an exotic feel to it. The perfect dish when the weather starts to turn a little cooler.

Simple enough to be part of your regular menu and works well when you are entertaining too. Interesting as a concept and you can create a lot of drama around it. Takes away from the fact that you have made just one dish- tops my cheat sheet. A DIY (Do it yourself) main course customised to everybody's palate- can it ever get better? As the host it allows you to ready most of the stuff earlier. No last minute frying and stirring, leaving you free to mingle with the guests/focus on the starters.

I had first sampled Khow suey at a friend's place, many moons ago. I vividly remember that lunch session and the novelty around this interesting dish. We had finished the meal with light, fluffy and lip smackingly, delicious mango gateaux- easily the best I have ever had.

The Khow suey version I make is leaner, uses no oil and the curry gets done in one easy step- assemble the ingredients and simmer. Then sit back, relax and enjoy your party.

Ingredients

60 mins   4-8 ppl

- Boneless chicken: 1 kg
- Garlic: 1 tbsp, finely chopped
- Onions: 3, finely chopped
- Ginger: 1 tbsp, finely chopped
- Jeera (Cumin) powder: 1 tsp
- Dhania (Coriander) powder: 1 tsp
- Tomato puree: 4 tbsps
- Chilli powder: 1 tsp
- Thin coconut milk: 2 cups
- Thick coconut milk: 2 cups
- Water: 1.5 cups
- Salt: to taste, about 2tsp
- Thin egg noodles: 500 gms

Method

1. Grind the ginger, garlic, onion, cumin, coriander with a little water to a fine paste.
2. In a pan, put the ground masala along with tomato puree and 1 cup water.
3. Bring to boil and then simmer till the masala is cooked.
4. Add the chicken and let the masala coat the chicken.
5. Add the chilli powder, salt and thin coconut milk and simmer till the chicken is tender (this should take about 10 minutes).
6. Add the thick coconut milk and check seasoning.
7. Chicken curry is done.
8. Boil noodles and keep aside.
9. To assemble, (this is my favourite part, makes this dish really unusual and interesting) serve boiled noodles in soup plates/bowls, pour the chicken curry over it and let the guests choose their topping.

Note:
Accompaniments could include fried onion flakes, fried garlic flakes, chopped green chillies, chilli flakes, hard boiled eggs (quartered), lemon wedges, finely chopped spring onion, finely chopped green coriander, finely chopped cucumber(de-seeded), basic sev (savoury topping) -yes, the same one that is used for Chaat(Indian street food) and some garlic chilli paste. Use some or all of them. Delicious!

CHILLI CHICKEN
An all-time Chinese favourite

In the 70's and 80's, a plethora of Chinese restaurants started mushrooming all across India. Limited fare, spiced up to suit the Indian palate and rich, deep fried dishes dotted the menu. Every nook and corner and every small town seemed to have sprung up a Chinese restaurant almost overnight. Later, as people started becoming more discerning, these restaurants evolved and now you get some really good Chinese restaurants in India. When we lived in Calcutta, more than a decade ago, Chinoiserie at the Taj and later Mainland China were two of my favourite places for Chinese food. However, the prices being steep, it was not a place you could go to every week. So we had to improvise and make some of the dishes at home. One item on the menu at every possible Chinese restaurant was 'chilli chicken.' I am not sure if the Chinese are aware or even eat this dish. Every Chinese restaurant in India has it on its menu. The menus may evolve, the restaurants may become spiffier but the chilli chicken is there for good! This recipe is my take on the ubiquitous chilli chicken.

Ingredients

90 mins 8 ppl

Boneless Chicken: 2 cups cut into small 2 inch pieces.
Corn starch: ¼ cup
Soy sauce: 3 tsps
Ginger: 4 inches
Garlic: 8 cloves
Green chillies: 2 large
Oil: About 2 cups for frying

Onions: 2 large cut into long thin slices
Tomato sauce: 2 tbsps
Vinegar: 1 tbsp
Simal Mirch(capsicum): 1 large cut into long thin slices
Salt: to taste

Method

1. Wash the chicken and keep aside
2. Grind the chillies, garlic and ginger into a fine paste. Add it to the chicken and mix well.
3. Add 2 teaspoons of soy sauce and half teaspoon of salt to the chicken and mix well.
4. Add the corn starch to the chicken and mix till all the chicken pieces are well coated.
5. Heat the oil in a deep pan. Reduce to medium heat and drop the chicken into the oil and fry.
6. Make sure that you don't overcrowd the pan, frying the chicken in batches of 6-8 at a time.
7. After all the chicken is done frying, put them on a blotting paper and keep aside.
8. Take a fresh pan. Heat 1 teaspoon of oil and fry the onions till they turn glassy.
9. Add the capsicum and fry for 5 more minutes.
10. Add the vinegar, a quarter teaspoon of salt, 1 teaspoon of soy sauce and the tomato sauce.
11. Immediately add the chicken and stir gently till it is well coated with the onion capsicum mixture. Serve hot with noodles or by itself as a snack.

Note:
Chicken thighs or breast pieces work the best for this recipe.

CHICKEN STEW
Easy, one pot chicken and vegetable casserole

This is yet another of those wholesome, one dish meals that I keep writing about; the ones that are nutritious and get done without too many ingredients or too much fuss. Chicken stew is a dish made on a cold, wintery/rainy evening. You throw in a couple of things into the pressure cooker; add a few more after opening it and you are done. Yes, it is that simple and as with baking, pressure cooking, apart from being time and fuel efficient, ensures you can do other things while your food is cooking (cock your ears for the whistle and turn it to low flame or switch it off depending on how long the dish needs to cook). And then the pressure cooker needs a cool off time which gives you an additional 5/10 minutes to get some more work done.

I typically use all the chicken pieces (neck and other bony pieces), that nobody likes eating as curry, to make the stew. I store these separately in the freezer and use them for soups and stews. The stew is a thick flavoursome broth together with the crunch of fresh, seasonal greens.

Ingredients

Chicken: 300 gms
Onions: 2, quartered
Beans: 5, cut into 1 inch long pieces
Carrots: 2, cut into 1 inch long pieces
Potatoes: 4, peeled and halved
Peas: ½ a tea cup
Tej patta(Bay leaf): 2
Kali Mirch(Whole pepper): 6

Salt: 1 tsp (or to taste)
Water: 5 cups
Freshly ground kali mirch pepper: 1 tsp
Capsicum: ½ capsicum cut into small cubes (The capsicum is a more recent addition at the suggestion of a friend. I add the capsicum towards the end, gives the stew a nicer flavour)

 60 mins   **8 ppl**

Method

1. Pressure cook the chicken pieces together with quartered onions, bay leaves, whole pepper, potatoes,1 teaspoon salt in about 5 cups of water. Give it one whistle and let the cooker cool naturally.

2. Open the lid and add the carrots, beans, peas. Put it back on the stove without the lid and let it simmer for a few minutes. Let the vegetables cook in the chicken stock for a while. Don't overcook them; they should be a little crunchy when you finally bite into them.

3. Once the vegetables are cooked, add the capsicum and some freshly ground pepper. Cook for another two minutes.

4. Serve piping hot with brown bread and herbed butter

Note:
Store the leftover chicken stew in the refrigerator (try and cook this in larger quantity to ensure you have some of it leftover). Next day heat up the stew, add some boiled noodles to it and voila, you have your very own Thukpa. thukpa is a hearty Tibetan noodle soup. It is a wonderfully nourishing and warming dish and is a like a fuller bodied stew. I was lucky to sample it in a Tibetan home (thanks to a really wonderful host) during a trip to Ladakh. I also use the stock for pulao and to season curries.

P.S: And did you notice there is just no oil in that dish. That does not take away from the flavour or taste. You have my word for it.

CHICKEN SHAMI KEBAB
A melt in your mouth kebab, pairs well with wine

One of the legacies of the Moghul Empire is definitely the rich repertoire of meat based dishes that they introduced; from biryanis to haleems to kebabs. I personally love kebabs but do not like pieces of meat or chicken, that invariably get stuck in my teeth. While using skewers to make kebabs, the prep work, marination, getting the perfect texture becomes complex and time consuming. So in that respect I find Shami Kebabs much easier. I love shami kebabs as the meat here is mincemeat and just melts in the mouth. The use of lentils as a binding agent gives it a nice, almost creamy texture that is delightful.

Ingredients

15 mins   4 ppl

Mincemeat: 2 cups (Chicken or goat meat. I have used chicken for this recipe)
Chana daal (Bengal gram): ½ cup
Kali elaichi (Black cardamom): 6
Hari elaichi (Green cardamom): 12
Dalchini (Cinnamon sticks): 4
Haldi (Turmeric powder): 1tsp
Salt: to taste

Ginger, freshly grated: 2 tbsps
Garlic paste: 1 tbsp
Green chillies, chopped: 4 large
Dhania (coriander) leaves chopped: ½ cup
Oil for frying
Onion: 1 medium sliced thin for garnish
Lemon: 1
Oil: 1 tbsp for mince

Method

1. Take a pressure cooker and add 1 tablespoon oil.
2. Once the oil is hot, add the cardamoms, cinnamon and sauté for half a minute.
3. Add the grated ginger, garlic paste and chopped green chillies and sauté for about 3 minutes.
4. Add the meat and the daal and sauté till the minced chicken is well cooked (about 10 minutes).
5. Put ¼ cup of water and salt and pressure cook for 8 minutes. Remove from fire and cool.
6. Remove the lid and check the mixture; it should be dry and sticky. If not, just put it back on medium flame and cook till almost all the water evaporates.
7. Let the mixture cool. Put the mixture in a blender or food processor and blend till it becomes a smooth paste. Add chopped dhania and mix well.
8. Take lemon sized balls of this mixture and flatten to form kebabs.
9. Shallow fry in oil and serve immediately with lemon wedges and sliced onions.

Note:
Sometimes, the kebabs may break while frying if the water content is high. If this happens, add some gram flour to the kebab mixture and shape and fry as usual.

DHANIA CHICKEN
Chicken entree in coriander leaves

Potluck dinners are quite popular amongst our friends. The etymology of the word pot-luck appears in 16th century England, and was used to mean 'food provided for an unexpected or uninvited guest, the luck of the pot'. Interestingly to the Irish, a potluck was a meal with no particular menu. Everyone participating brought a dish for all to share. The term comes from a time when groups of Irish women would gather together and cook dinner. They only had one pot so they cooked the meal together with whatever ingredients they happened to have that day.

For my friends and me, potluck is a convenient way to have a lot of fun. Each one of us gets a dish so the hosts are able to enjoy their party too. Everything tastes good in a potluck party with each one of us having put in all our effort into just one dish. This is quite in contrast to when you are preparing the entire meal by yourself and your attention gets divided among several dishes. Also, at the end of the meal everybody gets to carry back a little bit of the leftovers and as the host you are also saved from eating them for the next three days.

This is a dish that I typically carry to our potluck dinners. It is quick, uses no oil and goes equally well with roti and

Ingredients

60 mins   6-8 ppl

Chicken: 1 kilo

Tomato Puree: 1 cup

Dhania (coriander) powder: ½ cup

Red chilli powder: 1 tsp

Sugar: ½ tsp

Ginger garlic paste: 2 tsps

Salt: 1 tsp or to taste

Water: 1 cup

Dhania (Coriander) leaves: 1 cup, finely chopped

Garam Masala: 1 tsp (Blended spice made by pounding whole spices like cinnamon and cardamom in equal measure)

Method

This is the part I like the best. It is just one step. Almost like baking with the additional advantage of tinkering with the dish, half way through.

1. Mix all the ingredients (except the coriander leaves) together. Add a cup of water. Bring the gravy to a boil and let it then simmer, covered for about 20 minutes/till done (stir occasionally).

2. Switch off the stove, open the lid, add the coriander leaves and mix well.

3. Serve hot.

Note:
This dish always reminds me of a friend who would order it each time he visited Bar- B- Q on Park Street, Kolkata. Incidentally this is also the place where I sampled dhania (coriander) chicken for the first time.

MURGH KALI MIRCH
North Indian black pepper chicken

Murgh Kali Mirch is a famous chicken dish from Punjab. Is a close second after butter chicken. The star ingredient or the predominant spice is freshly pounded pepper which gives the dish its unusual flavour. The spiciness of pepper is beautifully balanced by the creaminess of curd.

There are multiple ways to prepare this peppery chicken dish, including a leaner variation without the cream. I had sampled a version of this dish, for the first time, at a friend's place. Had loved it and wished there had been a little more gravy to lick. This one does leave you wanting more.

I love dishes that need only to be marinated and then simmered. Once you have got the proportions right, it almost seems like the dish cooks on its own. Leaving you free to tend to the ones that need you to stand and stir for hours.

I prefer to cook my chicken with the bones; pieces turn out to be more succulent. I reserve the boneless ones for salads, pasta and sandwich spreads where you just can't have it any other way.

Ingredients

marination time		
3 hrs	2 hrs	6 ppl

Chicken: 500 gms

Onion: 2 to 3 medium sized onions, finely chopped

Thick Dahi (Yogurt): 4 to 5 tbsps

Sabut kali mirch(Whole pepper): 8 to10 pods

Ginger-garlic paste: 1tbsp

Salt: To taste, about 1 tsp

Sugar: 1/4 tsp

Ghee (Clarified butter) or Oil: 1 tbsp

Garam masala: 2 green cardamom and 1 inch stick of cinnamon (grind them with the pepper).

Cream (optional, but let me tell you that this is one dish where cream makes a difference to the consistency and taste. So maybe, just this one time, you can add the cream): 1 to 2 tbsps

Dhania (Coriander)leaves: ½ cup, finely chopped

Method

1. Beat the dahi with salt, sugar and the ginger garlic paste (adding a bit of sugar to the marinade ensures it does not curdle on heating).

2. Add the chicken pieces in the marinade (prick the pieces with a fork for the chicken to soak in the marinade). Keep the mixture in the refrigerator and let it sit for at least 4 to 5 hours. If you are in a hurry, make do with about 30 minutes of marination time.

3. Heat a cooking pan and add the oil/ghee. Once the oil/ghee gets heated, add the onions and fry till they turn glassy. Then, add the chicken pieces with the marinade and the ground whole spices and let it simmer for about 30 to 45 minutes. Keep stirring it from time to time, turning the pieces around.

4. Once the chicken is almost done add the cream (if using cream) and finely chopped coriander.

5. Serve hot with a roti and pulao. Makes a good accompaniment for Biryanis too.

Note:
An ideal main course dish when you are entertaining, this super quick creamy chicken is sure to be liked by your guests.
A drier version, made with boneless cubed chicken could serve as a starter akin to chicken

MUTTON VINDALOO
A spicy mutton preparation with strong vinegar flavouring

Vindaloo is a traditional Goan recipe inspired by the Portuguese but has travelled to my kitchen via Mumbai, Kerala and Chennai. It has taken the friendship route. I love recipes that have been handed over to me by friends (sometimes begged, borrowed or stolen as well). To start with, these are recipes that I have sampled in either their homes or lunchboxes; reminiscent of some happy times. To start with, these are recipes that I have sampled in either their homes or lunchboxes; reminiscent of some happy times. So even before I begin, I know what the end product would taste like. Unlike following just a recipe with this one you have the end in mind through the journey. Also, every time I follow the recipe, I remember my friend, and now with technology at hand I message to tell them that the dish has just been cooked. If I am lucky, I manage a photograph before it has been devoured. And finally, with most recipes I end up making it more often than the source of the recipe. Some friends have even threatened to charge royalty.

The key ingredients for a vindaloo are vinegar, mustard and garlic. Culinary history points to the use of wine in the original Portuguese recipe which was replaced by the local ingredient vinegar to create the same level of sourness. It has a fiery, red colour with a taste to match. Myriad of flavours and a must try for all meat lovers.

Ingredients

60 mins   4-6 ppl

- Mutton: 1 kilo
- Vinegar: 2 tbsps
- Red chillies: 20, soaked and de-seeded
- Ginger: 2 tbsps, finely chopped
- Tomatoes: 6, chopped
- Garlic: 2 tbsps, finely chopped
- Onions: 4, chopped
- Dhania (Coriander) powder: 2 tbsps
- Salt: To taste
- Jeera (Cumin): ½ tsp
- Oil: 2 tbsps
- Methi (Fenugreek): ½ tsp
- Mustard: 1 tsp
- Haldi (Turmeric): ¼ tsp
- Sugar: 2 tsps
- Hot water: ½ cup

Method

1. Grind together ginger, garlic, dhania powder, red chillies, mustard and fenugreek with the vinegar to a fine paste.

2. Heat oil in a kadai (wok). Add the onions and sauté till light brown. Next, add the chopped tomatoes and cook till they start to release oil. This should take about 10 minutes.

3. Add the ground masala paste and continue sautéing till there is no smell of raw ginger or garlic.

4. Add the mutton; toss it around in the kadai so that the masala coats the mutton. Add the salt and sugar. Mix well.

5. Next add the hot water (ideally half a cup per kilo of mutton but you could add more if you would like runny gravy). Pressure cook for about twenty minutes, initially on high flame and after the first two whistles put it on low flame.

6. Let the pressure cooker cool down naturally.

7. Serve hot with Malabar parathas or steamed rice. I alternate between the two and it tastes great each time.

Note:
Can be made ahead of time and tastes best the next day. You can also make the vindaloo paste and freeze in single use lots. Should stay well for a couple of weeks, if kept in the freezer.

MEAT LOAF
Ground, seasoned meat baked as a loaf

This recipe is dedicated to my paternal grandfather, Nana. He often quoted the famous phrase 'a pound of flesh' from the 'The Merchant of Venice'(Shakespearean play). That it was mostly in non-food related contexts and had something to do with his fights with granny is another story. Like the rest of the family, grandpa loved food and I think we get our foodie genes from him. He travelled across the world and had sampled different kinds of cuisine very early in his life. His food stories were a delight, he managed to create excitement around every day dishes. 'Pish pash' was one such creation- and until my brother found it on the menu of a daak bangla (referring to the times of the Raj) buffet, we had assumed grandpa had cooked up the dish, quite literally and figuratively, and given it a creative name.

Compared to baking bread or cake this one is a sitter. In terms of impact a perfect 10. The tri-coloured pie-mince, egg yolk and egg white look amazing. It tastes delicious too.

Ingredients

Mutton mince: 500 gms
Onions: 3, finely chopped
Breadcrumbs: ½ cup or 100 gms
Ginger garlic paste: 1 tsp
Vinegar: 1 tsp
Boiled eggs: 3
Raw egg: 1
Salt: to taste
Olive oil- 2 tbsps

90 mins   4 ppl

Method

1. Heat the oil in a pan and fry the onions till they turn light brown. Sprinkle some salt over them and let them cool.

2. In a bowl, add the mince, raw egg, ginger garlic paste, vinegar, bread crumbs and mix well. Add the onions and mix again.

3. Now take a loaf tin, line it with some oil or butter. Divide the mince mixture into two. In the tin pat one half of the mixture to form the bottom layer of the meat loaf. Next shell and place the boiled eggs in a row to form the middle layer. Cover completely with the remaining mince. Shape and compress to get rid of any air gaps.

4. Bake at 200 degree centigrade for close to an hour. Initially with only the bottom coil on and for the last twenty minutes with both the top and bottom coils.

5. Once done, let the meat loaf rest for about 15 minutes. Remove from the pan and slice evenly.

6. Take a bow when the accolades begin.

Note:
Ideally, serve this with a clear soup and some stir fried vegetables. Leftovers make for a good sandwich filling.

SPAGHETTI WITH MEAT BALLS
Meat balls in a tomato gravy served over spaghetti

There is something about being able to make a dish from scratch. When you cook a dish starting with basic, raw ingredients, you 'stay lifted longer'. You feel a kind of mastery over the dish. A 'yes, I have nailed it' feeling. It also allows you to customize the dish- sugar/spice/salt are all to taste (your family's taste) and of course it is fresher and you stake your claim on the entire dish.
But sometimes a dish can be so elaborate that it intimidates. Until recently, I cooked this dish with store bought meatballs. But now, I brave it and with some excellent results. And of course, the accolades feel good. Like the giant leap I took when I swam to the deep end of the pool.

Ingredients

2 hrs   6 ppl

For the meat balls
Mutton mince: 500 gms
Onions: 2 to 3 finely chopped
Garlic: 4 to 5 pods, minced
Bread: 4 to 5 slices (1.5 cups when cubed)
Milk: ¼ cup
Thyme: 1 tsp
Eggs: 2
Olive oil: 1 tbsp to be added to mince mix
Oil for frying: 5 tbsps
Salt: to taste
Kali mirch(Pepper): to taste

For the tomato sauce
Tomato: 8 to10 medium sized ones
Sugar: 1/2 tsp
Garlic: 2/3 pods minced
Italian seasoning (Oregano): 1 tsp
Red Chilli flakes: 1 tsp
Salt: to taste

For the Spaghetti
Spaghetti: 200 grams
Olive oil: 1 tbsp.
Salt: to taste
Water: 12 to 14 cups

Method

1. Boil spaghetti in 12 to 14 cups of water, 1 tablespoon olive oil and salt. Cook a little kacha (al dente). Drain water and keep aside. Reserve a cup of the starchy water for the sauce.

2. Meat balls. Trim sides and cube bread. Pour milk over the bread and leave to soften. Next, add all the mince ball ingredients and mix well to form dough. Make little round balls- anywhere between 15 to 20 balls. Shallow fry the balls in batches, turning them to evenly brown. Spread on paper towel to drain excess oil.

3. Sauce. Blanch and puree tomatoes. Heat oil and fry garlic till it changes colour. Add the pureed tomatoes, sugar, salt and seasoning and let it simmer for 10 to 15 minutes. Add the pasta (spaghetti) water (this gives it a nice, glossy texture), the meat balls and further cook for about 10 minutes.

4. To plate: Make a little spaghetti nest. Add a generous helping of the sauce and meat ball over it. Could garnish with chopped coriander and grated cheese. Contrast of colours makes this dish look really appetising.

Note:
Take slow, measured bites and savour each mouthful. Allow your tongue to play a wee bit longer with the succulent, juicy meatballs that have hungrily soaked up the sauce. And once done, pat yourself on the back and say, 'I did it'.

MOUSSAKA
Mince with potatoes and brinjal

For me, writing about food is therapeutic. It goes way beyond recipes, cooking and eating. It captures food memories, lets me reminisce about old times, reconnect with friends, helps me relax, inspires me to cook more, makes me feel more confident to experiment and more. In short, it makes for a happier me.

This recipe is yet another family favourite. I first sampled moussaka at a friend's place. A good friend and a wonderful cook. Someone who serves 'patishapta' (a traditional Bengali sweet) with a rich plum sauce, and layers her cheese cakes with 'notun guder mishti doi' (sweet curd preparation with jaggery). Over the years she and I have exchanged recipes, indulged in a lot of food talk but the one recipe that I instantly associate with her is moussaka. Moussaka is a three layered main course Greek dish. Yes, the name does make you feel curious to know a little more, but it is the taste, the combination of all those various flavours that tips the scales. You could also use regular leftover keema (mince) cooked the Indian way.

Ingredients

- Keema (mince): 500 grams
- Onions: 2, finely chopped
- Tomato puree: 3 to 4 tbsps
- Garlic: 6 flakes, chopped fine
- Potatoes: 4
- Brinjals: 1 large (without seeds)
- Oil: 1 tbsp (I use olive oil)
- Eggs: 2
- Dahi (Yogurt): 200 gms
- Oregano: 1 tsp

2 hrs   **6 ppl**

Method

1. Boil the potatoes and cut them into thick roundels. Also, cut the brinjal into thick roundels and shallow fry them with a little bit of salt.

2. Heat some oil, add the finely chopped onion and fry till it turns glassy. Next, add the garlic and fry for a few minutes. Add the mince and sauté for 4 to 5 minutes. Next, add the tomato puree, salt and oregano and continue to cook. Cover and cook for 10/15 minutes. Please note that the mince would continue to cook even after you have assembled the moussaka and put it in the oven to bake.

3. Once the mince is done start layering the dish. Use a deep bottom dish as there would be six layers in all. Use potato as the bottom layer, top with brinjal and then the cooked mince. Repeat. Do not press the layers down. There should be some gap for the egg and curd mixture to seep through.

4. Next beat the curd and egg with some salt and pepper. Pour over the potato, brinjal and mince layers. Allow it to settle down.

5. Bake at 200 degree centigrade for 30 to 45 minutes with both upper and lower coils on. The dish should brown lightly.

6. Serve with a clear soup and some garlic bread/bread sticks.

Note:
If making it as part of your entertainment menu, I would recommend making the mince, boiling the potatoes and shallow frying the brinjals, a day earlier. You could assemble and set the dish to bake about an hour before your guests are scheduled to arrive.

SAAG GOSHT
Spicy, tender meat stewed in a spinach sauce

This is a leaner variant of the popular mutton dish that is cooked with spinach. Saag gosht (mutton cooked with spinach) has its origins in Punjab (North India). In fact, to me this recipe is a cross between a mutton stew and curry. Simple and really easy to prepare recipe; you just need to put everything into a deep kadai (wok) and then let it simmer. It takes over an hour to cook; the benefit of slow cooking is that the meat becomes incredibly tender and the flavours infuse better. So, please don't take the easy route of pressure cooking this- you will end up with a sloppy mess.

This is perfect for those cold wintery evenings; winter is also the time of the year when you get the best greens. As the dish cooks by itself with almost no effort on your part, you could even plan it for a weekday supper. Given that it is a stew with very Indian flavours, it lends itself to both an Indian as well as continental spread. And even at the cost of repeating myself, I have to say that this a wholesome, healthy one dish meal.

Ingredients

2 hrs   4 ppl

Mutton (Goat meat): 250 gms
Onions: 3 medium sized, finely chopped
Palak (Spinach): 2 cups, finely chopped
Dahi (Yogurt): 1 cup
Ginger: 1 tbsp, finely chopped
Garlic: 1 tbsp, finely chopped
Jeera (Cumin): 1 tsp
Dhania (Coriander): 1 tsp
Green chillies: 2, finely chopped
Dalchini (Cinnamon): 1" stick
Tej patta (Bay leaf): 2
Elaichi (Cardamom): 2
Water: 3 cups
Salt: 2 tsps or to taste

Method

1. Place the mutton, onions, ginger, garlic, jeera, dhania, green chillies, dalchini, tej patta, elaichi and the water in a kadai. Place the kadai on high flame till the water starts to boil. Then let it simmer, cover and cook till the mutton is tender. This would take close to an hour.

2. Next, add the spinach and cook for a few minutes only. Make sure the spinach stays bright green and perky. Whisk the dahi so that there are no lumps and add. Mix well and remove from fire.

3. Serve hot with rice, roti or bread.

Note:
This is such a flavoursome dish that no one will notice the absence of oil. Try and choose meat pieces with bones as they enhance the flavour and texture of the dish. In fact you could even make this dish with just the bones. The spinach is not added until right till the end so as to retain the bright, green colour of the leaves.

As with all meat dishes tastes even better once you let it mellow in the refrigerator for a day or two; the meat pieces soak up some more of that fragrant broth.

MUTTON CURRY ROGAN JOSH
A mildly flavoursome goat meat curry

My husband is rather experimental with food and has always been the guinea pig, right from my early days of cooking. However, when it came to mutton, he liked it cooked only the traditional Odia way. Thanks to this dish, I can now proudly say that I have a convert. This new variant (years of being a marketer) adheres to my husband's mutton curry codes (some more marketing jargon) – fiery, red colour with an oily consistency to the gravy.
I have to thank my friend, in whose house I first sampled this tasty mutton curry. I discovered two wonder ingredients that she had added to the dish- a rogan josh masala and tomato ketchup. I now regret scoffing at meat masalas for so many years. Always regarded them as quick fixes where you ended up compromising hugely, on flavour and taste. This dish also made me realize how undervalued tomato ketchup, used primarily as a snack accompaniment, is. But here, it gives the gravy a richer red colour and an almost glossy finish. Some very easy steps and dollops of patience. And no, that is not a contradiction. It always amazes me that one extra ingredient or step produces something so different.

Ingredients

marination time: 4 hrs 60 mins 4 ppl

- Mutton (Goat meat): 1 kilo
- Onions: 4 to 5 medium sized, finely sliced
- Dahi (Yogurt): ½ cup
- Ginger garlic paste: 2 to 3 tbsps
- Lal mirch (Red chilli) powder: 1 tsp
- Haldi (Turmeric) powder: ½ tsp
- Sugar: ½ tsp
- Salt: 2 to 3 tsps (or to taste)
- Garam masala: 1 tsp
- Tomato ketchup: 1 tbsp
- Rogan josh masala: 2 to 3 tbsps
- Mustard Oil: 4 to 5 tbsps
- Tej Patta (Bay leaf): 2
- Potatoes: 4, halved

Method

1. Prepare a marinade of the ginger garlic paste, curd, chilli powder, turmeric powder, ¼ teaspoon sugar, garam masala, tomato ketchup and salt. Whisk well together. Add the meat pieces to the marinade and turn them over a couple of times so that the masala coats the pieces evenly. Cover with a cling film. Leave it in the refrigerator for a couple of hours or overnight.

2. Remove the mutton from the refrigerator about half an hour before you start cooking, so that it is at room temperature. Heat the kadai (wok). Add the mustard oil to it and let it smoke. Add the remaining ¼ teaspoon of sugar. Once the sugar starts to caramelize and turns a brown colour, add the sliced onions and stir them around on high flame for a couple of minutes.

3. Next, add the mutton, sauté for a few minutes. Add the meat masala, bay leaves and sauté till the oil separates (would take you a good 45 minutes to an hour). Add the potatoes and toss them around with the mutton.

4. Transfer to a pressure cooker, add water. Cover with the lid and cook for close to 20 minutes. On high till you get the whistle and then on medium heat for the next 15 minutes or so. Allow the cooker to cool down naturally.

5. Serve hot with rice and a salad.

Note:
-You could use sunflower oil if you are repulsed by the smell of mustard oil but the dish gets its characteristic flavours from the mustard oil, I am afraid. I am generous with my oil only when it comes to cooking mutton.
-The meat masala is the deal clincher and I am glad it is now available quite easily in most supermarkets.
-To make the garam masala freshly pound the green cardamom and cinnamon. Store bought garam masalas just doesn't have the flavour. If feeling too lazy to pound, use 2 to 3 whole cardamoms and 1 inch cinnamon stick.

RAILWAY MUTTON CURRY
A dak bungalow meat curry

This recipe, as the name suggest is from the times of the British Raj. Dak bunglow cooking refers to Anglo-Indian food that was the result of the efforts of some innovative Indian khansamas (cooks). They took aspects of British cuisine and amalgamated them with Indian spices and methods of cooking. So soups seasoned with lal mirch (red chilli) or jeera (cumin) or pot roasts marinated in garam masala. Also, much talked about, is the British mashed potato which in contact with the Indian spices took the now familiar form of chops and cutlets. The food these chefs created, was thus familiar in terms of form, for the British and yet very Indian when it came to the flavours; just a little milder. Over the years, these dishes have become more Indian than British.

Railway mutton curry was served in first class compartments and railway refreshment rooms during the times of the Raj. Believed to have been created because an English army officer though tempted by the flavours could not quite mouth the spicy Indian mutton curry. So the helpful cook reduced the heat with some coconut milk and served it up. And thus, was born 'railway mutton curry'. The tamarind in the recipe serves as a natural preservative and helps the dish stay fresh for hours, making it perfect for that long train journey.

Ingredients

marination time: 4 hrs 60 mins 4 ppl

- Boneless mutton (Goat meat): 1 kilo
- Onions: 3, sliced
- Potatoes: 3, peeled and cubed
- Curry leaves: 15
- Garlic: 8 flakes, finely chopped
- Ginger: 1 inch, finely chopped
- Haldi (Turmeric) powder: ½ tsp
- Salt: 2 tsps or to taste
- Jeera (Cumin) seeds: 2 tsps
- Dhania (Coriander) seeds: 2 tsps
- Oil: 4 tbsps
- Lal mirch (Red chillies): 8, de-seeded
- Coconut milk: 1 cup
- Imli (Tamarind) pulp: 2 tbsps
- Hot water: 4 cups

Method

1. Grind the jeera, dhania, red chillies, ginger and garlic to a fine paste. Keep aside.

2. Heat the oil in a kadai (wok). Add the curry leaves and sauté for about a minute. Next, add the sliced onions and let them brown. Add the mutton and fry till the mutton changes colour; this should take about 4 to 5 minutes.

3. Add the red chilli paste and cook the mutton in this paste by 'bhunoing' it (sauté on high flame, stirring it constantly). Add the hot water and salt and continue to cook; initially on high flame till the water starts to boil and then cover with a lid and let it simmer till almost done. Add the coconut milk and tamarind pulp and cook for 5 to 7 minutes. There should be no raw smell of tamarind in the dish.

4. Serve hot with rice.

Note:
- Ideally, meat should be cooked over high heat to seal the juices and then on low heat till tender. Simmering on low heat helps the meat to retain its moisture, juices and tenderness.

RICE AND PILAF

LEMON RICE
Tangy rice cooked with lemon juice

Lemon rice is one of the most popular rice preparations from the Southern part of India. Really easy to put together when you are in a hurry. Already cooked or steamed rice is mixed with lime juice, seasoning and peanuts.

Lemon rice always reminds me of train journeys. If your co-passengers hailed from Tamil Nadu (a state in the southernmost part of India), they were sure to be carrying lemon rice with them. I was told by some of them, that the rice stayed fresh for longer with lemon acting as the preservative, tasted good even when cold and the spicy, tangy taste helped relieve some part of the monotony of a long train ride. This tale, of course, comes from an era where everybody travelled by train, eating food bought from restaurants/ kiosks was frowned upon and there was very little hygienic food available on railway platforms.

Ingredients

15 mins   4 ppl

- Cooked rice: 3 cups
- Lemon Juice: 3 tbsps (one lemon should suffice)
- Oil: 1 tbsp
- Split Urad daal (Black lentil skinned): 1 tsp
- Chana daal (Bengal gram skinned and split): 1 tsp
- Mustard seeds: 1 tsp
- Curry leaves: 1 sprig (20 leaves)
- Hing (Asafoetida): A pinch
- Haldi (Turmeric): ½ tsp
- Peanuts: Fistful (roasted or fried)
- Green chillies: 1, finely chopped
- Red chillies: 2, whole

Method

1. In a small frying pan, heat oil and add the mustard seeds. Once they splutter, add the red chillies, chana and urad daals and fry on medium heat till the daals change colour.

2. Next, add in the chopped green chillies. Lower the heat and add the turmeric powder and asafoetida.

3. Finally, add the curry leaves.

4. Turn off the stove and add the cooked rice, salt, juice of one lemon and mix well with a spatula

5. Serve hot with a spicy chutney and papad (poppadum).

Note:
Lemon rice also makes for a hassle free lunch box option and interestingly, is liked by both the young and old. Lemon adds the tanginess, while the tempering imparts the aroma and the peanuts add the crunch to this simple rice delicacy. And for my generation and beyond, memories of some delightful co-passengers we met during our long train journeys. People, who were more than happy to share their lunchbox and bits about their lives with us, to them I remain ever grateful for adding this staple to my repertoire.

CHICKEN PULAO
Rice cooked with chicken

This recipe is for people who are strapped for time and still want to serve a hot, delicious, cooked meal. Chicken pulao is typically the meal that follows my chicken stew dinners. Just save some of the stew for later and you get your flavoursome pulao done in a jiffy. Cooking with leftover essentially means that a large part of your job is already done.

Pulao is a rice based dish that often includes ingredients like vegetables and/or meat. Long grained rice varieties like Basmati are preferred for pulao. Basmati cooks faster and the ensuing pulao has a light, fluffy texture. Basmati tends to be preferred by people from the Northern part of India. Further, these loyalists claim Basmati is gluten-free, low in fat, contains all eight essential amino acids, folic acid, is very low in sodium and has no cholesterol.

My preference for Basmati is led more by its visual appeal- light, delicate and separate grains. A treat to the eyes as also to the taste buds.

Ingredients

soaking time		
1 hrs	30 mins	4 ppl

- Basmati Rice: 2 cups; soak for at least an hour
- Onions: 3; finely chopped.
- Potatoes: 4 halved
- Salt: to taste
- Chicken stew: 2 cups
- Oil/Ghee (Clarified butter): 1 tsp
- Biryani masala: 1 tsp. The masala lends a nice flavour to the pulao. In fact, you can smell the pulao long before you have opened the pressure cooker.
- Hot water: 1 cup

Method

1. Heat the ghee in a pressure cooker. Once the ghee heats up, add the onion. Sauté till the onion turns glassy. Add the potatoes, cover for a little while.

2. Next, add the rice and stir for a few minutes. Followed by the chicken stew, 1 cup of hot water, biryani masala, and salt. Close the cooker, cook on high flame and let it give out one whistle. Then cook on low flame, for another 5 minutes. Switch off the cooker and let it cool down naturally.

3. Serve hot with a cucumber, onion and tomato raita (curd relish).

Note:
A no fuss, quick cook pulao. The leftover stew reduces the cooking time without you having to compromise on taste. The biryani masala would also work well with a basic jeera (cumin) rice recipe, would add dollops of flavour.

And cooking with leftovers made me feel 'so clever'. Loads of appreciation with only half, no one third the effort. The woman is smarter, that's right!

TIRANGA PULAO
Tri coloured vegetable pulao

This one is an Independence Day special made in the colours of the Indian National Flag. The typical way to make this tri-colour rice is to cook three types of rice separately- palak (spinach) rice for green, carrot rice for the colour saffron and then combine it with some plain rice in the middle for the final effect. Looks really nice and goes well with the Independence Day spirit.

My version is a quicker, oil free (in keeping with the freedom theme), one dish wholesome meal. The combination of brightly coloured vegetables makes this a visual treat and nobody seems to miss the butter or ghee typically associated with a pulao.

Ingredients

60 mins   4 ppl

Basmati Rice (choose the long grained variety): 1.5 cups

Onions: 2, finely chopped. You could also use Shallots- about 8/10 peeled

Ginger: 1 tbsp finely chopped

Tomatoes: 2, finely chopped. Choose large ones; this is a key ingredient when you are cooking with no oil

Carrots: 1, cut into 1/2 inch long pieces

Beans: 10, 1/2 inch pieces

Baby Corn: 4, 1/2 inch pieces

Tej Patta (Bay leaves): 2

Jeera (Cumin seeds): 1 tsp

Elaichi (Green Cardamom): 2/3

Lime juice: 1 tbsp

Salt to taste

Hot Water: 3 cups

Method

1. Soak the Basmati rice for about an hour before you start cooking. Do follow this step for all Pulao.

2. Heat a non-stick kadai/wok. Dry roast the bay leaves, cumin seeds and cardamom till fragrant.

3. Add the onions, ginger and tomatoes and cook for a few minutes till the tomato turns soft.

4. Add the vegetables, rice, salt and mix well. Cook for five minutes.

5. Transfer to a pressure cooker, add 3 cups of hot water (this helps cook the rice faster and prevents it from sticking) and lime juice. Close the lid of the cooker and let it give out one whistle. Switch off the cooker and let it cool down naturally.

6. Serve hot along with cucumber-tomato- onion raita. Enjoy ,Would like to salute the master chefs from whom I picked up all my no-oil and lean cuisine tips.

Note:
-With lean cooking there are two basic rules:
-Be patient because a good part of the cooking needs to be done on low flame. Some steps may need constant stirring. Try and use a good non-stick cookware.
-The food is low on oil but high on flavour so some of the dishes(like this one) need a lot of ingredients- basic everyday use ingredients but quite a few nevertheless.

CURD RICE
Yogurt rice

This is a recipe that is close to every South Indian's heart. It is truly comfort food. A perfect meal according to people from the south of Vindhyas, needs to end with curd rice. And never mind, if the cuisine being otherwise served is Chinese.

When we moved to Chennai, we watched with initial amusement, as every buffet worth its salt had curd rice as part of the menu- star hotel dinners, birthday parties, potlucks. It was omnipresent and seemed to be relished by all.

Outsiders to the region confessed that in their early years in the city despite serving elaborate and exotic fares at their parties the guests went back unhappy because there had been no 'thayir sadam' (local name for curd rice). So, a little grudgingly, they had started to add it to their menus.

Till we relocated to Chennai, I used to think that curd rice would be one of the easiest dishes to make. How hard can it possibly be to mix rice with curd and then temper with the regular curry leaves, mustard seeds? There was obviously a lot that I did not know. When I tried making it my way, I ended with hard rice that stood separate from the watery curd (unlike the real one where the rice was soft and the consistency homogenous). Mine also turned sour when I carried it in my lunchbox, whereas that, which my Tamilian colleagues brought every day, did not. I tried cooking the rice softer, varying the quantity of curd and still it did not work. And then I swallowed my pride, dumped my pre-conceived notions and just asked for help.

This curd rice recipe comes from the masters, and over the years has been perfected by, yours truly.

Ingredients

Cooked rice: 3 cups, cook the rice really soft
Milk: 1 cup
Dahi (Yogurt): 1 cup
Ginger: 1 tsp, finely chopped (optional)
Oil: 1 tsp
Urad daal (Black lentil skinned): 1 tsp
Mustard seeds: 1 tsp

Curry leaves: 10 leaves
Hing (Asafoetida): ¼ tsp
Red chillies: 2
Salt: to taste
Dhania (Coriander) leaves: 1 tbsp (optional)

15 mins   4 ppl

Method

1. Take the cooked rice in a bowl. Mash it slightly with the back of a spoon. Add the milk to it and leave it for a few minutes to cool.

2. Once the rice has cooled down, add the curd to it and mix well.

3. Next, heat oil in a kadai. Once the oil is hot add the mustard seeds. Once the mustard sputters add the red chillies, asafoetida, urad daal, ginger (if using) and fry on medium heat till the daals change colour..

4. Finally, add the curry leaves.

5. Turn off the stove and add the tempering to the cooked rice. Add salt to taste.

6. Garnish with coriander leaves and serve at room temperature or chilled, with lime pickle.

Note:
As a variation you could add pomegranate or grapes. Subtle, but splendid flavours and a calming, soothing taste; I quite agree now that curd rice is indeed a wonderful way to end any meal- vegetarian or non-vegetarian.

CORN METHI PULAO
Corn and Fenugreek casserole

Food that is beautiful to look at tastes better than food that isn't. So sometimes I find myself adding ingredients just to add more colour to a dish. It invariably adds to the taste and flavour. Like sprigs of fresh mint to a fruit salad; some red chillies to a raita garnish, the vibrant red contrasting with the creamy white texture and the subtle chilli tempering enhancing the overall taste. It is a lot of fun to keep adding different coloured ingredients to a salad. Red, green and yellow bell peppers can make an ordinary tomato cucumber salad look exotic. I suspect they are primarily added to salads for the colour. Cherry tomatoes, black grapes, green olives have a similar impact. Toss in some Feta cheese or boiled eggs and the colours stand out even more strongly against the white backdrop.

And then of course there is the more difficult task of colour coding an entire menu. Making sure that no two dishes look the same. This also serves as a screener to ensure all the dishes use separate base ingredients and taste different.

Pulao like salads allows for a lot of colour play. With corn methi pulao one did not have to try very hard to make the dish look visually appealing. White rice, yellow corn and green methi leaves together create a colourful platter. Depending on your personal palate preference you could tinker with the corn and methi proportions. Some carrots and beans would add even more colour but perhaps make it a little lower on distinctiveness.

Ingredients

Basmati rice: 1 cup (when it comes to pulao Basmati works best)
Kali Mirch (Pepper): 3
Dalchini (Cinnamon): 1/2 inch piece
Laung (Cloves): 2
Elaichi (Green cardamom): 2/3
Onion: 1/2 sliced
Methi (Fenugreek) leaves: 1 cup chopped fine
Sweet corn kernels: 1/2 cup
Haldi (Turmeric) powder: 1/4tsp
Salt to taste
Ghee/Oil: 1 tbsp. (I would suggest you stay with ghee, in combination with the whole spices imparts the pulao with a lovely flavour. In fact you could just serve rice flavoured with ghee and whole spices. Cook that in mutton stock and it turns into Yakhni)
Hot Water: 2 Cups

30 mins 2 ppl

Method

1. Soak the rice for about 30 minutes to an hour. This makes the pulao more 'khila khila' that is keep the grains separate. Soaked rice also cooks faster.

2. Heat the ghee in a pressure cooker; add the whole spices and onion slices. Fry for a few minutes.

3. Then add the methi leaves, corn kernel, turmeric powder and stir. Add the rice, salt and mix well. Fry for a few minutes.

4. Finally add 2 cups (a little less than double of the rice quantity) of hot water. Hot water helps the pulao cook faster and prevents it from sticking.

5. Pressure cook for 1 whistle and let the cooker cool down naturally. Serve with some plain dahi/yogurt and a green salad.

6. This is a quick pulao sans the endless fuss of peeling and chopping. Perfect for those busy weekday dinners.

CHINESE KONJI
Chinese rice porridge

When I think of my culinary journey I am always reminded of the cookery show 'Yan can cook'. This was a show in the early 90's where a Chinese man would clumsily try and cook some really simple stuff. He was funny, dropped things as he cooked and made you laugh as you watched the show. The overt message was "If Yan could cook so can you". I too started off rather disastrously in the kitchen, managing to burn a fried egg, surviving on 'Cup-O- Noodles' for the first two weeks of married life. Cup noodles are of the instant variety and all you had to do was pour hot water- those days I thought even that required skill- getting the quantity of water right, ensuring you kept the cup covered for exactly three minutes, mixed with a certain deftness to get the seasoning to coat the noodles evenly. My husband has enough stories to fill our cocktail evenings.

Over the years I have pored over recipe books, learnt from friends/relatives/cookery shows and sometimes even had long chats around food with perfect strangers. I learnt how to cook, then experiment and finally innovate. Willing tasters who also double up as my cheerleaders in the form of my husband (who has had to 'stomach' quite a bit) and my children helped.

Since I started my journey with noodles anything Chinese always has a special place in my heart and kitchen. The Chinese Konji recipe has been passed on to me by my husband's aunt. It is easy to cook, easy to digest and nutritious. Tastes delicious too.

Ingredients

40 mins   6 ppl

Basmati Rice (Take long grain rice): 1 Cup

Chicken stock- 5/6 cups or Stock cube: 1 to 2

Shredded Chicken: 1/2 cup

Shrimps: 1/2 cup (optional)

Soya Sauce: 1/2 tsp per serving

Egg: 1

Salt to taste

Mix of vegetables like beans, carrots, green peas and mushrooms: 1/2 cup

Method

1. Pressure cook the basmati rice with 5/ 6 cups of water (or stock). If using water add the stock cube while pressure cooking. 6/7 whistles, should be a gooey gruel like consistency

2. Open the pressure cooker (add hot water if the consistency seems too thick), add the shredded chicken, prawns and vegetables and allow them to cook for a couple of minutes (should not take more than 2/3 minutes). Add salt to taste(remember to keep the salt low as soya sauce which is added as garnish is high on salt)

3. Add a well beaten egg, stirring continuously

4. Transfer into individual bowls, add a dash of Soya sauce

5. Serve hot

Note:
Best had on cold winter or a rainy day. For my family this is comfort food. For those of you watching the calories this is a no oil dish and the quantity of rice being consumed per person is less than quarter of a cup so low carbs too.

You could have it just by itself or serve it with a spicy chicken dish or stir fried vegetables.

CHOW CHOW
Noodles in a chicken and vegetable broth

Chinese food continues to be my all-time favourite. I can have it any time of the day. You will often catch me eating omelettes stuffed with leftover chowmein for breakfast (a trick I learnt from my mom). I add boiled noodles to my salads, stuff chilli chicken pieces into kathi rolls, serve pakodas (vegetable fritters) with soy dipping sauce. In short, anything remotely Chinese goes for me. I can never seem to have enough of it.

Chow chow is a dish that I have eaten for as long as I can remember. It is a delicious main course Chinese dish. The story goes that we sampled this dish in a restaurant in Kolkata (then Calcutta). Mom came back home and tried her own variation of it. Through trial and error she finally arrived at this one. Seems easy, but it's hard to get the crunch of the vegetables, the flavours and the consistency of the sauce right. If you have chicken stock readily available this dish gets done in a jiffy. Though it is not as well known as chowmein, I like it apart from its taste, for being a meal by itself.

Ingredients

60 mins 4 ppl

- Onion: 2, quartered
- Capsicum: 1, cubed
- Carrots: 2, chopped
- Beans: 10 to 12, sliced into 1" pieces
- Cauliflower: 6 florets
- Cabbage: ¼, chopped into large pieces
- Corn flour: 1 tbsp
- Boiled and shredded chicken: 1 cup
- Chicken stock: 2 cups
- Soya sauce: 1 tsp
- Vinegar: 2 tsps
- Kali mirch (Pepper): 1 tsp
- Salt to taste
- Noodles: 1 packet
- Oil: 1 tbsp
- Sabut kali mirch (Whole Pepper): 4

Prepare chicken stock by pressure cooking 4 to 5 bony chicken pieces with 5 cups of water, one onion quartered, salt and whole pepper. Give it 4 to 5 whistles. Let the pressure cooker cool naturally. Strain and use the water as stock.

Method

1. Parboil (half cook) the carrots, beans, cauliflower and keep aside. Similarly boil the noodles and keep aside.

2. Heat oil in a kadai (wok). Sauté the onions. Then add the carrot, beans and cauliflower and stir on high flame. Do not overcook the vegetables; they need to retain their crunch. Add the capsicum, cabbage, shredded chicken, noodles, some salt and mix well.

3. Mix the chicken stock with the vinegar, soya sauce, corn flour, salt and pepper. Add to the kadai.

4. Mix well and allow the sauce to coat the noodles and vegetable combine. You are done.

5. Serve hot.

Note:
- You could also use leftover chicken stew to make a similar dish. Sauté onions, add noodles, add the leftover stew, corn flour, soya sauce, vinegar, salt and pepper.
- For a vegetarian version use vegetable stock (prepared by boiling one cup of vegetables in about three cups of water and straining the liquid to form the stock) and skip the shredded chicken.

BASIL RICE
A Thai Favourite

Our trip to any Thai restaurant is incomplete without ordering basil rice. We ask for it at every Thai place that we go to. Although each restaurant has a slightly different basil rice recipe, a constant is the spicy tanginess of the dish and rice bursting with the strong herbal flavor of basil. There is an interesting story about Basil In India, a kind of basil also known as "tulsi" is thought to be a holy herb – to be revered and worshipped. The fact that someone would use this herb to cook and that too use it to flavor meats was nothing short of blasphemy. Due to this reason, traditional rice or meat recipes from India never have basil as a cooking ingredient and it is mainly found in Thai cooking. I did a little bit of research and realized that the Indian herb tulsi is of a different species than the Thai basil. So one does find people growing Thai basil in India nowadays so that they can cook different Thai recipes.

I experimented with this dish at home mainly to try and reduce the sodium and oil content that we typically find in Thai restaurants, at the same time trying to retain the flavor and texture of the original dish.

Ingredients

Long grained rice: 2 cups
Butter: 2 tsp
Olive oil: 1 tbsp
Shallots: ½ cup
Onions: 1 medium, chopped fine
Garlic: 4 pods (chopped fine)

Red chilli flakes: 1 tsp
Basil leaves: 1 cup coarsely chopped
Chicken: ½ cup chopped into small cubes
Fresh lemon juice: 1 tbsp
Salt: To taste (about 2 tsp)

30 mins   6 ppl

Method

1. Wash the rice and keep aside.
2. Take a large pan and heat 1 tsp of butter and the olive oil.
3. Add the chilli flakes and onions and stir till onions turn glassy. (do not let them brown)
4. Add the chicken and stir till chicken is cooked.
5. Add the shallots and wait for about 1 minute and then put the rice and half of the chopped basil.
6. Stir the rice so that all the ingredients are mixed in.
7. Add 4 cups of water, salt and cover till the rice is almost done.
8. Add the remaining basil, 1 tsp of butter, lemon juice and gently mix in.
9. Cover and cook for another 5 minutes, till the rice is all done.
10. Remove from fire and serve hot.

Note:
You can add 1 tsp of fish sauce at the end to enhance the flavor. To add even more flavor you can cook the rice in chicken stock instead of water. Vegetarians can make this dish by substituting vegetables for chicken and adjusting the cooking time accordingly.

KANIKA
A semi sweet, traditional East Indian pulao

Kanika; a dish very typical of Orissa. It is usually made for auspicious accassions like a pooja or a wedding. One of the staple offerings of 'Abhada' – the traditional rice and vegetarian curries offerred at the Jaganath temple at Puri every day, this dish is very delicate in its flavor. When people ask me to describe what this dish tastes like, I am at a loss for words. Even though this is a rice dish, it is neither a pulao nor a kheer. It is not a halwa or a fried rice. The taste is semi sweet so it really defies all the typical categorizations associated with rice. Sadly, not many people make this dish anymore. Food at weddings is now catered from the best hotels in town and making this at home, just for a meal is uncommon. It is a very traditional dish that I am afraid may become extinct very soon. So here is my version of the dish.

Ingredients

45 mins   6 ppl

Basmati rice: 1 ½ cup
Yellow moong (Split yellow peas): 1tbsp
Ghee (Clarified butter): 1 tbsp
Raisins: 20 – 25
Whole cashews: 20
Black elaichi (cardamom): 3
Green elaichi (cardamom): 3
Dalchini(Cinnamon) stick: 1 inch

Laung (Cloves): 4
Jaiphal(Nutmeg) powder: A pinch
Bay leaf (tejapatta): 1 large
Sugar: 2-4 tsps
Salt: to taste
Haldi(Turmeric): ½ tsp
Fresh grated coconut: 2 tbsps
Water: 3 cups

Method

1. Wash and soak rice for 1 hour. Drain all water and spread on a plate.
2. Wash the moong daal and keep aside.
3. Sprinkle the turmeric and mix it gently with rice. Allow to dry for 1-2 hours.
4. Heat the ghee in a deep and thick bottomed vessel. Add the raisins and cashews. Fry till cashews are golden brown and the raisins puff up (about ½ a minute).
5. Remove and keep aside.
6. Add the whole spices (cardamom, cinnamon and cloves) to the remaining oil and stir for 20 seconds. Add the dried rice and daal and fry it gently for 3 minutes.
7. Add 3 cups of boiling water to the rice. Add salt.
8. Allow to cook on a low to medium flame.
9. Stir gently at an interval of 4-5 mins.
10. Once rice is almost done, add the sugar, nutmeg powder, cashews, raisins, fresh coconut and mix them gently with the rice.
11. Once the water dry and the rice is done, remove from the flame and serve immediately.

Note:
Usually this dish is had all by itself or at the beginning of a traditional meal like a first course, without adding any daal or curries to it.

CHUTNEY & DIP

TOMATO AND AAM PAPAD CHUTNEY
Sweet tomato and mango relish

Chutneys help spice up an otherwise boring meal. There is no limit to the number of chutneys that can be made from any vegetable/fruit/herb/spice or a combination of them. My Mom recently combined some sweet grated mango chutney with hung curd and a handful of fresh mint (from my kitchen garden). Like with everything else when it comes to food the possibilities are endless. Most chutneys also double up as sandwich spreads, dips. I also add leftover pudina (mint)/dhania (coriander) chutneys into gravies to spice them up.

Tomato chutney or chaatni as it referred to is the most common form of chutney in the Eastern part of India; a quintessential part of Bengali wedding menus. The lavish spread usually finishes with tomato chutney and papad. You literally lick your fingers to the finish. The best way to enjoy this chutney is to savour it bit by bit, to let the sweetness with a tinge of sour pervade through your senses.

Adding aam papad or aam shoto as it is called in Bengali (mango leather) or khajur (dates) makes the chutney more flavoursome. Aam papad adds body and gives the relish a nice sweet and sour taste.

Ingredients

30 mins   6-8 ppl

Tomato: 1/2 kilo, medium sized tomato
Aam papad (Mango fruit leather): 5 or 6 strips, chopped into small bits
Sugar: 4/5 tbsps.
Salt: To taste
Panch Phoran: 1 tsp, Panch phoran is jeera (cumin), saunf(fennel), kalonji (nigella), methi (fenugreek) seeds, sarson (mustard) seeds mixed in equal quantity
Oil: 1 tsp
Whole Jeera (Cumin): 2 tsp

Method

1. Heat oil in a kadai/wok. Once the oil heats up add the panch phoran and let it sputter. Next add the tomatoes and cook till they soften. This should take about 10 minutes.

2. Then add the sugar and let it dissolve completely. Followed by the salt. Finally add the aam papad.

3. Dry roast the jeera seeds and coarsely grind them. Sprinkle it over the chutney. Let the Chutney cool. Store in the refrigerator.

4. Serve cold.

Note:
Chutneys stay well for days and are healthier than pickles which tend to be high on oil, that killer salt and spices. Ideal when you are entertaining as you can make it a day or two early.
Do not add any water while cooking the chutney otherwise you will not get the sticky texture.

GREEN PAPAYA RAITA
A quick yogurt salad made of green papayas

I like papayas. Actually I love ripe papayas, unlike my sister who used to proclaim with great drama that all papayas were "kadarjiya" (terrible in Odia) when she was little, much to my grandparent's amusement. Frankly one can't blame her. Raw green papaya hardly has any taste and is quite a bland fruit waiting to ripen. The ripe papaya is quite sweet, mushy and has a distinct smell which some people like and some really cannot stand. This recipe however, uses raw papayas. Raw papaya is a low calorie vegetable with a rich source of phyto-nutrients, minerals, and vitamins. It is also used as a meat tenderizer in many Indian recipes.

The raw papayas here is used to make a simple raita (yogurt salad) that serves as a quick and easy side dish especially during summers. Great for those who want to eat healthy.

Ingredients

10 mins   6 ppl

Green Papaya: 1 cup, finely shredded after removing the dark skin and seeds if any.
Dahi (Yogurt): 1 cup
Salt: ½ tsp
Sugar: ¼ tsp
Fresh desiccated coconut: 2 tsp for garnish
For the Garnish / Tadka
Ghee (Clarified butter): 1 tsp
Green Chilli: 1, chopped fine
Mustard seeds: 1 tsp
Curry leaves: About 12

Method

1. Boil 1 cup of water and remove from fire.
2. Soak the shredded green papaya in hot water for 5 minutes.
3. Mix salt and sugar with the yogurt.
4. Strain the green papaya and squeeze out the excess water and mix into the yogurt.
5. In a pan put the ghee and the chopped green chillies.
6. Add the curry leaves and mustard seeds.
7. Once the mustard seeds start to crackle, remove from fire and pour on top of the yogurt mixture.
8. Add coconut and mix. Serve immediately.

Note:
This is a really healthy quick summer relish. If you want to make it spicier, add 1 tsp of mustard paste to the yogurt mixture. This dish does not store well and needs to be served immediately.

DAHI BAINGAN
Fried brinjal in yogurt sauce

This is a typical Odia dish. Every time I make dahi baigan (brinjal in yogurt), it brings back memories of Odia weddings of yesteryears where this would invariably appear as a part of the menu. Those were the times when weddings would be held mostly at homes, food would be painstakingly made by cooks specializing in wedding feasts and the planning would take days to put it all together. The recipe uses fried eggplant. I have tried lower calorie versions using baked brinjal but it really doesn't taste the same. So make it once in a while if you have to, but definitely try the original version given here.

Ingredients

Baingan (Brinjal): 4, medium sized
Dahi (Yogurt): 1cup
Salt: 1 tsp
Sugar: ¼ tsp
Oil for frying

For the garnish / tadka
Ghee (Clarified butter): 1 tsp
Green Chilli: 1 chopped fine
Mustard seeds: 1 tsp
Curry leaves: About 12
Fresh desiccated coconut: 2 tsps

chilling time
+4 hrs

10 mins

8 ppl

Method

1. Cut the brinjal into medium size pieces
2. Deep fry in the oil till they are golden brown.
3. Sprinkle ½ teaspoon salt and keep aside.
4. Mix remaining salt and sugar with the yogurt.
5. After the brinjal becomes cooler, mix into the yogurt.
6. In a pan put the ghee and the chopped green chillies.
7. Add the curry leaves and mustard seeds.
8. Once the mustard seeds start to crackle, remove from fire and pour on top of the yogurt mixture.
9. Add coconut and mix. Refrigerate for four hours and then serve cold.

Note:
This is a nice and tangy side dish which is very filling as well.

PEANUT CHUTNEY
South Indian savoury peanut relish

Chutneys spice up any dish. The southern part of India eats a lot of idlis (rice cakes) and dosas (savoury lentil crepes). Typically these are accompanied with a spicy lentil soup called Sāmbhar and a platter of chutneys. My take on chutneys is a little different. I treat it as a side dish. Like you would treat a salad or raita.

They make great leftovers too. You can use it as an appetizer topping, a sandwich spread or eat it as a palate cleanser at the end of a satisfying meal when you are craving just that something tangy to round up the meal.

This one is my favourite. I love peanuts and this is a great way to have them. It can also be a substitute for coconuts in traditional chutneys and many people these days are making that switch due to health reasons. This recipe tastes particularly good the next day as a sandwich spread. So you could eat it the first day with dosas or idlis and the next day with your sandwich.

Ingredients

10 mins   6 ppl

Roasted Peanuts: 1cup
Imli (Tamarind) paste: 2 tsp
Green chillies: 1 chopped fine
Salt: 1 tsp
Sugar: ¼ tsp
Oil: 1 tsp
Ginger: 1 inch cube cut into small pieces
For the Garnish / Tadka
Ghee (Clarified butter): 1 tsp
Green Chilli: 1 chopped fine

Method

1. Soak the tamarind in 2 tablespoons of warm water and keep aside for 5 minutes.
2. Heat oil in a pan. Add chillies, ginger and fry till it is brown. Add the roasted peanuts and mix on medium heat.
3. Add the sugar and salt and remove from the fire.
4. Strain the tamarind paste to remove the pulp. Strain well to get nice thick tamarind juice.
5. In an electric blender blend the peanut mixture and tamarind paste till you get a thick smooth paste.
6. In a pan put the ghee and the chopped green chillies.
7. Add the curry leaves and mustard seeds.
8. Once the mustard seeds start to crackle, remove from fire and pour on top of the peanut mixture.
9. Serve with idli or dosa.

Note:
When using as a sandwich spread, skip the tadka (tempering) part.

GUACAMOLE
A light fruity mousse

Guacamole is a Mexican dip that I truly love. This dip is something I cannot resist, even after knowing that a single serve of guacamole has almost 300 calories! It is a source of good cholesterol though, is what I tell myself when I indulge. Made of fresh green avocadoes, this dip needs to be consumed immediately after you make it. The moment you keep it out for some time, it just starts to turn brown and becomes quite unappetizing. Sure, store bought versions remain "verde" forever and ever, but I for one just don't like the taste of those super smooth synthetic tasting guacamoles and can bet my life on the fact that they must have added some weird chemicals to make them stay that way.

And why should I buy guacamole when the recipe itself is so easy to make? I like mine, chunky and tangy with a hit of lime. Experiment with the proportions and you can come up with your very own version of Guacamole. Ideally it should be served with some warm tortilla chips. But if you want to go all low calorie, serve it with some vegetable sticks...Can't promise that they will taste as good as chips but hey! all of us have to choose our poisons and stick with them...happy dipping!

Ingredients

Semi soft avocadoes: 2 (available in the exotic fruit section of any modern retail store)

Onion: ½ medium sized, diced into tiny pieces

Green Chilies: 2, cut into small pieces

Tomato: 1small, cut into small pieces

Lemon/ Lime: 1 large

Dhania (Coriander) leaves: 1 small bunch, chopped fine

Garlic: 3 large cloves, chopped fine

Salt: to taste (about ½ tsp)

Method

1. Cut the avocado into half.
2. Remove the seed and scoop out the pulp and put in a large bowl.
3. Add the onions, chilies, garlic and coriander.
4. Mix well, making sure that the avocado remains chunky
5. Squeeze lemon juice and add salt to taste.
6. Mix well and serve immediately with warm tortilla chips.

10 mins   6 ppl

Note:
Use semi soft avocadoes. The over ripe ones have a tendency to be brown inside and the hard ones don't mash well. Serve immediately and discard leftovers as they don't freeze or store well. If you make them right, you will not have any left over.

DESSERTS

CHOCO BANANA CAKE
Light chocolate & banana breakfast cake

I find myself baking almost every other day. Makes for a convenient snack option. Store in an airtight container inside the refrigerator. Microwave for about thirty seconds before serving for that freshly baked taste. So the cake could technically stay for days. That it gets polished off in less than twenty four hours is another story.

This cake always reminds of the Harry Belafonte banana boat song, one of Dad's favourite singers. We learnt to hum the songs even before we knew what the lyrics meant. Some of my favourites include Jamaican farewell, Come back Liza, Woman is smarter & Angelico Mamma gonna take you back. Actually almost all of them. These are songs with a soul and tug at your heart strings. My boys love these songs too. In fact, the older one suggested that since the inspiration for this dish is the "ripe" banana I must talk about Harry Belafonte who made the term famous.

Ripe bananas lying on the kitchen shelf meant it was time to bake a banana cake. Most recipes for banana cakes go "medium sized over ripe bananas". I got this recipe from a friend who said the cake was to die for. And well, she was not exaggerating. It is an interesting combination and one that works. Goes well with vanilla ice cream or fresh cream. My boys think it tastes quite good on its own. One cake they are quite happy to eat straight out of the refrigerator.

Ingredients

- Banana: 1 cup mashed
- Eggs: 2
- Oil: 1/2 cup
- Milk: 1/2 cup
- Warm water: 1 cup
- Maida (Refined flour): 1+ 3/4th cup
- Cocoa powder: 3/4th cup
- Sugar: 2 cups
- Salt: 1/2 tsp
- Vanilla essence: 1 + 1/2 tsp
- Baking soda: 1+ 1/2 tsp
- Baking powder: 1 +1/2 tsp

baking time: 1 hrs 30 mins 8-10 ppl

Method

1. Sieve together all the dry ingredients which include the flour, sugar, cocoa powder, baking powder, baking soda and salt. Keep aside.

2. Next whip the eggs with the bananas, add water, milk and oil. Mix well.

3. Fold in the flour mix little by little, stirring continuously ensuring that there are no lumps. The batter is really thin and the cake takes a little longer to bake. But definitely worth the wait. Pour into a greased tin. Bake at 200 degree centigrade for about an hour. For the first 40 minutes keep only the lower coil turned on and for the last 20 minutes bake with both the upper and lower coils turned on. This gives the cake a nice thin crust on the top and along the sides. Check if the cake is done by inserting a toothpick. The toothpick should come out clean.

4. Serve as dessert along with some fresh cream or vanilla ice cream.

Note:
Given the rich, dark colour of this cake you could also frost the cake with some powdered sugar, creates an interesting contrast.

DATE APPLE CAKE
A rich fruit and nut cake

Cakes are possibly the most popular form of dessert. They straddle different occasions with ease- ceremonial ones like birthdays/ anniversaries/ weddings, tea times, breakfast times, snack times at school and then all the in between times when you feel like a nibble or could do with something sweet.

The ingredients of this cake, apple and date combine, as well as the crust (cinnamon, sugar and nuts) make this a little different from the regular chocolate/vanilla fare. When you take a bite you can almost feel the burst of flavours in your mouth. As the cake starts to bake the aroma of apple and cinnamon makes the kitchen smell absolutely divine. Always puts me in a cheery frame of mind.

Store the cake in the refrigerator (if you can manage to make it last that long) and warm it for about 30 seconds in the microwave before you serve. It also goes well with fresh cream or ice cream. You can start your day with a slice of this cake and down it with a glass of milk or pack it in your lunchbox and relish it after a light lunch. So go ahead and indulge the taste buds.

Ingredients

baking time: 45 mins 20 mins   4-6 ppl

- Apples: 2 cups (chopped fine)
- Dates: 1 cup (again chopped really fine)
- Maida (Refined flour): 1.5 cups
- Sugar (Powdered): 1 cup
- Sugar (Granular): 1 tbsp
- Eggs: 2
- Vanilla essence: 1.5 tsp
- Baking soda: 1 tsp
- Baking powder: 1 tsp
- Butter: 1 cup
- Dalchini(Cinnamon)powder: 1/2 tsp
- Jaiphal(Nutmeg)powder (optional): 1/4th tsp
- Sliced almonds: 1/2 tbsp

Method

1. Sieve the flour together with the baking powder and soda. Keep aside.

2. Beat the two eggs with the vanilla essence until light and fluffy, Again keep aside.

3. In a large mixing bowl combine the powdered sugar and the butter (keep the butter out of the refrigerator for a couple of hours to make this step easier).

4. Once the butter and sugar have mixed well(should take about 10 minutes or so) start to add the flour and the eggs bit by bit- alternating between the two till you are done.

5. Next add the apples and dates. You could also add 1 tbsp of the sliced almonds or save all of it for the topping. Add the nutmeg if using.

6. Pour (now this is not really a pouring consistency cake) so just spoon it onto a greased dish. Flatten the top with a spatula.

7. Then sprinkle some granulated sugar, cinnamon and the sliced almonds over them.

8. Preheat the oven at 200 degree centigrade for about ten minutes and the bake the cake. Initially with just the lower coil for about 30-40 minutes and then with the upper and lower coils for another 10/15 minutes till the crust starts to look a rich, golden brown.

Note:
Baking most cakes just requires you to sieve the dry ingredients together, mix the wet ingredients and then assemble. Believe me it is therapeutic.

CARAMEL PUDDING
Steamed milk and egg pudding

During our growing up years desserts were a regular at dinner. Typically a custard with lots of fruits, different types of kheer or pudding. At the beginning of the meal we would ask: What's for dizzy pazzy? Dizzy Pazzy was our way of referring to the dessert. My sister with the sweetest tooth among us would very often skip the main course to save some of her appetite for the dessert. Dizzy Pazzy, can't recall how the term originated, you know how families have their private jokes, code language etc.

Coming back to the dessert. I did not have any favourites then. In fact I was not much of a dessert person, I loved the imlis, achars and khattai a lot more. Kheers were okay, custard tasted nice when it was chilled, puddings were a little unpredictable. Some days they would be just right: soft to touch, even textured, firm enough to be cut into individual portions and with a predominant vanilla flavour. Then there were other times when the pudding would have an eggy smell, the texture would be uneven (result of the cook being hasty about adding the egg to hot milk) and the consistency wobbly.

When I got married and set up home I did not make pudding, was not quite sure how to. Though when we dined out I would invariably order Caramel Pudding as dessert. I love the way restaurants plate the pudding- served as small individual portions with a wee bit of cream and a cherry on the top. And then my husband's aunt shared her recipe with me. Since then it has been a regular on my menu. My sons otherwise reluctant to eat eggs love pudding and I see it as a clever way to slip in the eggs.

Ingredients

chilling time: 2-3 hrs 30 mins 4-6 ppl

Milk: 3 cups

Sugar: 4 to 5 tsps. (If you prefer your desserts really sweet you could add a few more tsps.)

Eggs: 2

Vanilla Essence: 1 tsp

Sugar: 2 tsps to caramelize

Method

1. Heat the milk and reduce to 2.5 cups. This should take about 10/15 minutes.

2. Remove from fire and cool, then add the sugar and mix well.

3. Beat the eggs with Vanilla essence to a fluffy consistency. Add to the milk.

4. Take a small steel container and caramelize 2 tsps. of sugar (place it on the stove and keep stirring on high flame till the sugar turns a rich brown colour, turn the container around so that the sugar coats the base evenly). Let it cool.

5. Pour the milk and egg mixture into the container. Pressure cook without the whistle for about 15 minutes

6. Remove, let it cool and then refrigerate

7. To serve loosen from the sides and turn it over on a plate. Cut into individual slices and serve.

Note:
Kids love it as an after school snack, in between meals. Rarely had as dizzy pazzy though. Sigh!

LEMON POPPY SEED CAKE
Light citrusy, crunchy cake

Baking a cake is magical. To mix everything together and watch it take shape- no stirring no tweaking. I peep several times into the oven to watch the cake rise. It takes a few attempts to perfect the temperature setting (each oven being quite unique). Some cakes bake at 200 degree centigrade with just the lower coil on for 15/20 minutes and then at 150 degrees for the rest of the baking with both the coils working together. And then there are others which cook at lower temperatures for much longer.

This cake uses two fairly unusual cake ingredients, black poppy seeds (this is the differentiator) and lemon (zest into the cake and the juice onto the glaze). The poppy seeds provide an interesting pattern- they look lovely dotting the cake and give it a delightful crunch. The cake is mildly sweet which contrasts beautifully with the citrusy crust. Referred to as bread and the combination goes beautifully with both breakfast and tea times.

Ingredients

baking time
45 hrs

20 mins

4 ppl

- Lemon- 1 medium sized
- Maida (Refined flour) - 1.5 cups
- Baking powder- 1 tsp
- Eggs- 2
- Sugar- 1 cup
- Butter- 1 cup (if using unsalted butter do add 1/2 tsp of salt to balance out the sweetness)
- Sugar (powdered) - 1/2 cup
- Butter- 6 tbsps
- Milk- 1/2 a cup
- Black poppy seeds(Black khus khus)- 1/4th of a cup

Method

1. Mix all the dry ingredients together- flour, baking powder and salt (if using salt).

2. In a large bowl mix cream butter and sugar together. Add the eggs and mix one after the other and whisk until light and fluffy.

3. Alternate adding milk and the flour mixture till done. Stir in grated lemon zest and the poppy seeds.

4. Pour the batter into a greased baking dish and bake for 15/20 minutes at 200/220 degree centigrade with the lower coil on and for another 20 minutes at 150 degrees centigrade with both the upper and lower coils on.

5. Once done remove the cake onto a plate. Prepare the glaze by mixing the juice of one lemon with the confectioner's sugar. Poke a few holes in the cake and pour the glaze over it. Poking the holes lets the cake absorb the glaze better.

6. Let the cake sit for a few hours for the glaze to be soaked in completely. Cut the cake into large slices and devour. At this stage you typically go yummm!

Note:
This cake has a perfect balance of flavours and a refreshing summery feel to it. The glaze oozes right down keeping the cake soft and moist. In one word- delicious!

THAI BLACK RICE PUDDING
Rich pudding with black rice & coconut milk

I am no stranger to rice puddings or kheers as they are called in India. This rice pudding was truly an experiment that worked! One thing we used to notice in Thai restaurants was the lack of desserts on the menu. Even if they did, it would be just a simple ice-cream or a cake. I always wondered if that was the real reason why people from the Far East were mostly skinny.

Anyways, having a very sweet tooth, I would always look out for the desserts at the Thai restaurants. There is one which is pretty close to where we live called Nam. They serve the best purple rice I have ever had. It is a mildly sweet rice, served as a side dish. But it is sweet enough to qualify for a dessert. I found the texture and the colour very interesting. I chanced upon a bag of black rice at an Asian mart here and tried making a Thai type kheer out of it. What resulted has now become a family favourite.

Ingredients

60 mins   **8-10 ppl**

Black Rice: 1 cup
Coconut Milk: 1 cup
Condensed Milk: ½ cup
Sugar: ¼ cup
Water: 3 cups
Ghee (Clarified butter): 2 tsps.
Fresh desiccated coconut: 2 tsps for garnish

Method

1. Wash the rice and keep aside.

2. Boil two cups of water in a container and add the rice.

3. Wait for it to get cooked. Should take about 15/20 minutes. The rice should be semi soft and the water should have dried up.

4. Remove from fire. Add 1 tsp of ghee, sugar and mix well. Add the third cup of water, condensed milk, and return to fire and simmer on medium heat, stirring at regular intervals.

5. The mixture will begin to thicken with a pudding like texture.

6. Add the coconut milk and continue to stir.

7. When the mixture is sufficiently thick and the coconut milk is well blended into the mixture, remove from fire.

8. Add 1 tsp of ghee and mix.

9. Cool and serve with coconut garnish.

Note:
Black rice is available at gourmet food stores in India. Else you can use white rice for this dish. It won't have the brilliant purple colour but taste will be as good as its purple counterpart. You can make the pudding runny like a kheer or really dense like a pudding based on your preference. Rice cooker can also be used to make this dish. Make rice as per instructions on the cooker. Once the rice is done, follow the rest of the procedure from step 4 above.

BHAPA DOI
Steamed sweetened yogurt

Bhapa doi is a traditional Bengali festive sweet. It is the kind of Indian dessert that does not require any fancy ingredients and can be made quite easily at home.

This recipe has been passed on to me by a Bengali friend who spent many years in Europe in the late 80's when Indian food and especially desserts were neither popular nor easily available. Bhapa doi for her (and countless others) thus served as a convenient, easy to prepare, authentic Bengali dessert. I have made it umpteen times, tried variations of it including a bhapa doi Cheese Cake and passed it on to several other happy chefs. This is a never fail recipe and would Wow! your guests for sure.

Traditionally bhapa doi used to be steamed in a pressure cooker filled with little water. This recipe uses the oven method where the bhapa doi is baked in a water bath. Please do note that bhapa doi looks and tastes quite different from mishti doi which is another popular Bengali curd based dessert.

Ingredients

chilling time		
2 hrs	3 hrs	8-10 ppl

Dahi (Yogurt): 400 grams

Condensed milk: 400 grams/1 tin (if you don't like your desserts very sweet then use only 3/4th of the tin)

Kishmish(Raisins): 10/12(Optional)

Method

1. Make hung dahi. This is done by tying the dahi in a muslin (cheese) cloth and hanging it for a couple of hours till all the water drains out. When you open the cloth about an hour or two later the dahi should be thick and creamy.

2. Next mix the hung dahi and condensed milk together; lightly by hand. Add the raisins if using.

3. Bake on a double boiler or water bath at 140 degree centigrade for 1 hour.

4. Let it cool at room temperature and then refrigerate.

5. Serve chilled

Note:
I usually serve it with seasonal fresh fruits, goes best with mango. Looks best with a strawberry topping and in fact strawberry also offsets the sweet taste of bhapa doi. High on calorie but delicious to taste.

GULAB JAMUN
Milk solids dumpling in thick sugar syrup

During my growing up years there was an India Today article on Delhi Campus lingo. Years before the advent of mobile phones and sms language (brb, btw would have been dismissed as gibberish in an era where people spoke the Queen's language). The author had written with some amusement about college students getting into the habit of shortening everything and the traditional syrupy sweet gulab jamuns were thus being referred to as g jams. This was also around the time when burgers and pizzas were making their entry into India and so the Indian fare had to quickly re-invent itself. Nomenclature change seemed like the quickest and easiest to compete in times where anything Western was hip and happening. Yes, much has changed today (Jai ho!) and there is pride in everything Indian like never before.

I learnt making gulab jamuns from my friend. By the time I arrived at her place she had already done the basic preparatory work of soaking the sooji (semolina) and measuring out all the other ingredients. I was an eager and helpful assistant. I did the mixing, kneading and made the g jams under her expert guidance. The most difficult part was the "standing time" as my friend called it where you put the fried balls into the syrup and wait. It is hard and maybe the best thing for you to do is to go take a walk (literally).

Ingredients

Sooji (Semolina): 100 grams (3/4th cup)
Khoya (Milk solids): 250 grams
Sugar: Two cups, adjusted to taste
Refined oil: 1 cup
Elaichi (Green cardamom): 1 to 2
Patience: Plenty, especially towards the end

soaking time	standing time		
1 hrs	1 hrs	60 mins	8-10 ppl

Method

1. Soak the sooji in water- just enough to cover it, for about two hours. The sooji should have soaked up the water by the time you start the actual cooking.

2. Thaw the khoya in the microwave for about 30 seconds. Knead the khoya and sooji together for about 15/20 minutes. They should come together like a softer roti dough and there should be no lumps.

3. Make small balls out of the dough- you should get anywhere between 22 and 25.

4. Fry the balls in medium flame till they turn dark brown and keep aside to cool down.

5. Make the sugar syrup(this takes a while so I would suggest you let the sugar syrup simmer before you get started with the kneading) by adding the two cups of sugar to about three cups of boiling water, add the green cardamom, let the syrup thicken on low flame. When the syrup starts to thicken check if it is done by taking a little bit between your thumb and index finger(caution- hot)- as you try and separate your finger you should see a thin string kind of thing(" ek taar" as it called in Hindi) then you know it is done.

6. Drop the balls into the syrup and give it about an hour of standing time.
Store them in the refrigerator in an airtight container. These keep well for days. You could serve them with vanilla ice-cream or even custard, halve them and top with malai and nuts (like malpua). But I like my g jams just by themselves.

RASGULLA
Cottage cheese dumplings in sugar syrup

Growing up in Odisha, rasgullas were available in plenty. Every street shop round the corner was sure to have them. Most popular among sweets and lent themselves to any meal big or small. Rasmalais got made with leftover rasgullas and the extra syrup was the perfect accompaniment to parathas for breakfast.

When I got married and set up home in distant Chennai, what got peddled in the guise of 'Bengali sweets' was a far cry from rasgulla. So we had to contend ourselves with eating them only during our annual visits to Odisha. Then my husband's uncle from Canada taught me how to make them at home. I observed, assisted and watched closely. I learnt that he did not drain the water completely from the paneer (cottage cheese), that he kneaded the dough patiently and then took a little bit of it in between his palms and rolled them 'lightly' into a ball. He also dropped the balls quite gingerly into the syrup. And he seemed happiest when they were all gone in minutes.

Ingredients

kneading time		
30 mins	45 mins	6 ppl

Full cream milk for Paneer (Cottage cheese): 2 litres

Sugar: 1 cup

Sooji (Semolina): 2 tsp (1 tsp for every litre of milk)

Vinegar: 2/3 tbsps

Eliachi (Green cardamom): 2/3

Water: 4 Cups

Method

1. Boil the milk. Curdle it into paneer using the vinegar. Let it stand for about 5 minutes and then drain out the water. Don't let the paneer dry out completely else the rasgullas will turn out quite hard/chewy.

2. Add sooji to the paneer and knead the dough. Next take a bit of the dough and roll into little round balls. By this time your palms would be covered in oil- that means you are doing it right. Keep the balls aside. Two litres should get you about 30/40 rasgullas.

3. Make sugar syrup in a deep kadai or pressure cooker (minus the lid) by boiling 1 cup of sugar in about 4 cups of water. Add 2/3 green cardamom to the syrup.

4. Drop the paneer balls into the syrup one by one (give them one final roll before you drop them as this helps retain the shape). Let them boil for about 15 minutes- they should have become at least three to four times their original size.

5. Switch off the gas and let the rasgullas soak in the syrup.

6. Once the rasgullas have cooled down transfer into an airtight container and leave them in the refrigerator overnight.

7. Serve the following day or after they have been in the syrup for 6/8 hours. If that seems like a stretch do remember that most sweet shops make rasgullas at night and sell them the next day.

8. I usually stay almost glued to the spot and watch these little devils swell up in size. There is a sheer joy in watching the paneer balls metamorph into rasgullas.

BARFI
Dry cashew Brittle that stays fresh for weeks

Out of all the things I cook for potlucks, this is the dish that I get maximum "can we have the recipe please" requests for. Barfis are a type of traditional Indian sweetmeat that are almost like a dry fudge They can be brittle or soft and typically have a very long shelf life. This particular barfi is essentially a Cashew barfi, although it is very different from the store bought kajoo katlis. A friend of mine taught me this recipe and I added some ingredients of my own to make it more brittle and incorporate chickpea flour which I love. Although my husband refers to this heart attack on a plate, this is a sweet that I just can't stop making, eating and sharing! Easy to make and an instant crowd pleaser, you just can't go wrong with Kajoo (Cashew) Barfi.
And good luck with stopping at one!

Ingredients

30 mins   20 ppl

Sugar 2 Cups

Butter 2 Sticks (Approximately 2 cups)

Raw Whole Cashews 1 & 1/4 Cup

Grated Coconut : 1 Cup (Fresh or Frozen)

Dry non:fat Milk powder 1 Cup

Besan (Chick pea flour) 2 Tbsp

Method

1. Coarsely grate the Cashews.

2. Make sure that the butter is at room temperature, or else soften the butter (A quick 10 : 15 seconds in the microwave does it for me)

3. Mix all the ingredients with a spatula except the besan.

4. Put the mixture on medium heat and stir constantly, so that the mixture doesn't stick to the bottom. (This mixture burns pretty quick if it is not stirred)

5. After 15 minutes, sprinkle the besan on top of the mixture and stir again till it is well blended with the mixture. Continue to stir.

6. After some time (about 20 25 minutes) you will notice that the mixture begins to take on dough like consistency and starts to move together like a ball.

7. Let it cool for about 5:6 minutes.

8. Cut into squares or diamond shapes while it is still warm.

Note:
This Barfi tastes best when made fresh. However, it has a decent shelf life and you can store it for up to 7 10 days in an airtight jar.

NATURAL ICE CREAM
Fresh fruit ice cream

Remember that little rhyme we learnt in school, I scream you scream we all scream for Ice cream. I think all of us can vividly recall our initial ice cream experiences. The ice gola man Mama banned us from, the attempts at making ice cream at home with malai (clotted cream) and sugar, graduating to branded ones like Kwality Walls, Baskin Robbins, and Hagen Dazs.

But "home-made ice cream" in this day and age when you are spoilt for choice? Aren't there enough ready to eat ice-creams already? A yes and no to that. Yes, there are plenty of different types available in all shapes and sizes but no they cannot match homemade ice creams when it comes to retaining that fresh fruit flavour. I tried the strawberry version at my cousin's place (this is her Mother in law's recipe) years ago on a hot summer day and loved it. Since then I have made it with almost all fruits available though my personal favourite is mango. Make sure the fruit you choose is fleshy and sweet.

These frozen treats are easy to make; so smooth, creamy and luscious.

Ingredients

chilling time
12 hrs 30 mins 4-6 ppl

Fruit Pulp: 1 cup (Mango/Strawberry/Lychee/Guava/Kiwi)
Cream: 1 cup (if using malai or clotted cream add a little more)
Sugar: 1 cup (3/4th of a cup if the fruit is really sweet)
Milk powder: 1 cup
Milk: 1 cup
For the topping- 1 cup of the fruit, finely chopped

Method

1. Mix all the ingredients together and run it in the mixie for a couple of minutes
2. Freeze for 12 hours
3. Serve topped with fresh chopped fruits
4. This takes a little long to set so make it the afternoon before if planning to serve it for lunch and early in the morning if planning to serve for dinner. When you need to make larger quantities, do not double/triple the ingredients (you could go wrong on the sweetness and consistency). Instead make them in separate lots. Would be easier to serve too as children typically eat first followed by the adults.

Note:
And do make sure you have enough as most people including grownups would go in for a second/third helping. So next time you feel like an ice cream fix, just make it at home. It is so simple, just five ingredients and all of them in equal proportion. So make it in exactly the flavour you crave.

CHENNA PODA
Traditional vegetarian caramelized cheese cake

I have to narrate this funny incident that took place recently. A south Indian friend had called me over for a huge party at her place. I had promised to take some dessert for the party. I made a batch of Cashew Barfi and at the spur of the moment made a batch of a typical Odiya dish called Chena Poda for the party. The Chena Poda was a big hit. And most of her guests had not even heard of the dish let alone eaten it before. However, to my utter surprise, every time they asked for seconds, they used to burst into laughter. And they pronounced the dish as "China Poda"! After sometime it dawned on me that "Poda" in Tamil meant get lost. So they assumed that the name of the dish was China get lost instead of Chenna Poda, which literally translated meant burnt cottage cheese in Odiya!

Traditionally, this rustic dish involves making a thick mixture of fresh cottage cheese, sugar, a dash of sooji (cream of wheat which acts as a binding agent), shaping the dough as a cake, wrapping it in a special leaf and putting it in an earthen clay pot and baking it on high heat for hours. When it is ready to eat, the burnt leaves are discarded to reveal a dark brown caramelized layer outside and a nice brown caramel cheesy layer towards the middle of the cake, hence the name Burnt cheese or Chenna Poda. You really have to eat an authentic one in Odisha to taste how delicious the burnt layer truly is.

I do have to admit that however hard you try, the homemade ones are not half as good as the real thing. But then when one lives so far away, one can just experiment and hope to come as close to the real recipe as possible. So here it is, my version of Chenna Poda…. which to me will always remain THE most delicious cheesecake ever!

And good luck with stopping at one!

Ingredients

120 mins   4-6 ppl

Fresh Paneer(Cottage Cheese) or Full fat Ricotta Cheese : 2 cups

Sugar (Preferably brown sugar): 1 cup

Sooji (Cream of wheat): 2 tablespoon

Butter: 1 teaspoon

Elaichi(Green cardamom): 4 pods

Method

1. Take all the ingredients except the cardamom and mix well.
2. Remove the seeds of the green cardamom and crush them to a coarse powder.
3. Mix into the cheese mixture
4. Grease a baking dish with butter.
5. Pour the mixture (it will be a thick paste) into the greased baking dish.
6. Bake on 350 degree centigrade for an hour.
7. Broil on low for the last 5 minutes to get a nice brown top layer.
8. Cut into pieces and serve warm.

Note:
- I sometimes use 1/4th cup brown sugar and reduce the white sugar accordingly to get a nice caramel flavour as well as a warmer brown colour.
- Please use fresh cottage cheese if you don't get ricotta cheese.
- DO NOT use store brought Paneer blocks for this recipe.

KHUS KHUS HALWA
Poppy seed pudding

There are dishes that you might have eaten a long time ago but remember quite vividly. The ones, that bowled you over with the first bite. You were taken in by the taste or the flavour or possibly the whole concept. Maybe you never ate the dish again but thought about it very fondly several times over the years. Even long after memories of the person who had prepared the dish or the place where you sampled it have started to fade.
Being a foodie, there are quite a few that I can talk about. Let me start with 'Kewra kheer', delicious and unusual, from the regular elaichi (cardamom) one. An egg curry prepared by breaking eggs over already simmering gravy. Sandwiches on my first flight- large triangles with a thick slice of cheese in between, 'Tutti fruity' ice cream at Hotel Rebecca (lone restaurant in the town I grew up)-that memory made me order Tutti fruity ice cream for years afterwards. 'Rogan Josh', the highlight of our vacation in Kashmir, 'Roomali roti and Kebabs' from Pandara road during my first trip to Delhi. A baked crab in shell dish, prepared by a guest house chef in my little town. I just have to close my eyes to visualize these dishes and can almost feel their taste in my mouth. Some food memories do stand the test of time.
The dish in focus is 'Khus Khus halwa', sampled for the first time at a friend's place. Being from the East I was familiar with the usage of khus khus in curries and dry subzis. But a khus khus halwa? I was sceptical. But one mouthful and I was sold. Delicious, with the rich taste of khus khus and ghee combined. Loved the taste and helped myself to a generous second helping, despite the warning bells in my head.

Ingredients

Khus Khus (Poppy seeds): 100 gms
Ghee(Clarified butter): 4 tbsps
Sugar: 4 tbsps
Milk: 3/4th cup
Dry Fruits: 4 tbsps (Finely chopped)

soaking time		
7-8 hrs	45 mins	4 ppl

Method

1. Soak the khus khus overnight and grind to a paste with 2 to 3 tablespoons of water. Should be a semi solid paste (approximately about a cup).

2. Next heat the ghee, cook the khus khus in the ghee till done. Then add the milk and sugar and cook for a while. It would all need to come together. Should start to resemble Sooji (semolina) halwa.

3. Add the chopped dry fruits and serve hot.

Note:
Frequently Asked Questions
No, this does not require tons of khus khus. And no, this does not make you feel sleepy/dopey.
My friend tells me that Maharashtrians eat this halwa when they are fasting. To me this tastes more like 'feasting' food. Sinfully delicious!

TRADITIONAL COCONUT PODO PITHA
Traditional Odia rice cake with coconut

Podo pithas are a festival staple in Orissa. This rustic pitha is very different from chenna poda pitha featured earlier and less rich. Almost a breadlike texture, this pitha is semisweet in taste and is usually had with curries. We used to have this pitha long time back when my mom or grand mom used to make it for specific festivals like Prathamastami- a festival that celebrates the first born child in the family. Living in the US, I remembered this pitha during one of the festivals and asked my mom for the recipe, which she conveyed over phone. Traditionally this pitha uses jaggary and is baked in a coal oven wrapped up in thick leaves. I improvised and added brown sugar instead of jaggary and used an oven to bake the pitha. The results were pretty good.

Ingredients

soaking time +overnight | 60 mins | 8 ppl

- Rice: 1 cup
- Urad Daal (Black gram skinned): 1 cup
- Brown sugar: ¼ cup
- White sugar: ¼ cup
- Vegetable oil or ghee: ¼ cup
- Elaichi(Cardamom)powder: 1 tsp
- Salt: ¼ tsp
- Coconut slices: ¼ cup
- Baking powder: 1 tsp

Method

1. Soak the daal and rice in double the quantity of water overnight.
2. Use a blender and a little water to grind them into a thick paste.
3. Add sugar and oil and mix well.
4. Add baking powder and mix well.
5. Lastly add the thinly cut coconut slices, cardamom and salt and mix well.
6. Pour into a greased baking dish.
7. Bake in an oven (300 degrees) for 60 minutes.
8. Remove and cool.
9. Cut into large cubes to serve.

Note:
You can skip the sugar altogether to make a savoury version of this dish.

LOW FAT 'TIRAMISU'
A low fat take on a decadent Italian dessert

I am a part of a book club. Every month, we meet to discuss a book that we would have read during the month. I really look forward to these meetings and sharing my love of books with these like-minded friends. Every book club meeting is held at one of our homes and we switch it up every month so that everyone gets a chance to host a meeting. The meetings are typically held on a weekday evening and the host prepares a simple home cooked meal; usually a soup, salad and a dessert for other members to nibble on while we discuss the book. I always find it interesting to see how each host puts her own flair to the food and how the same salad or soup tastes different in different homes.

I had this dessert at one of our recent book club meetings. As soon as they brought out this yummy dessert, we just devoured the whole thing in minutes. I, of course had to know how it was made. Once I found out the ingredients and the procedure for making it, I was taken aback at how simple it was to make this dish and how few ingredients were needed. Although it tasted like the Italian dessert tiramisu, the ingredients were not your typical high calorie tiramisu ingredients. It has very few steps and uses just a couple of low calorie ingredients. Purists may argue that this dessert is not really tiramisu. I would argue back- If it looks like tiramisu, tastes like tiramisu……..it is tiramisu!

Ingredients

chilling time: 4 hrs | 10 mins | 8 ppl

Marie Biscuits: 24
Light whipped cream: 2 cups
Instant coffee: 2 tbsps
Sugar: 4tbsps
Chocolate powder: 1tbsp
Warm water: ½ cup

Method

1. Mix chocolate powder, light whipped cream and sugar till well blended and keep aside.

2. In a large bowl, put ½ cup warm water and coffee powder and mix well.

3. While the coffee mixture is still warm, dip the biscuit in it and quickly remove after both sides are coated with the coffee mixture.

4. Layer in a nice flat container.

5. Add a second layer with the whipping cream.

6. Again, add a layer of the dipped biscuits, followed by a second layer of cream.

7. Continue till all biscuits are over.

8. The final layer should be the cream layer.

9. Refrigerate for about 4 hours or even overnight if possible.

10. Serve cold.

Note:
You can see the nice biscuit layers when you cut into this dessert. The taste is very close to tiramisu although technically it is not. The low calories in this dessert compared to the real tiramisu (which uses ingredients like mascarpone cheese, whipped egg yolk), is an added bonus.

MONDA PITHA
Deep fried cream of wheat fritters, stuffed with sweet coconut stuffing

Growing up in India, one grew up with so many festivals, religious or otherwise, and myriad ways to celebrate them. Every province of India had their distinctive traditionsand customs. One common thread was the importance of food, specifically sweets, as a part of the celebrations. One just had to have something sweet to round up any celebration and no festival was complete without having some desserts to mark the occasion. Sometimes they were made as a religious offering, and some other times it was just a very complicated sweet that I suspect people made only during those special festivals as they would be too tedious as an everyday food. What ended up happening is that we associated some festivals with their characteristic desserts. Ganesh Chaturthi signalled 'Modaks', Onam-'Pal Payasam' and Eid- 'Sewai Halwa'. And in Orissa, we had 'Pithas'. 'Pitha' is the generic name for traditional Odia sweetmeats. This particular one always evokes childhood memories of festivals and visions of mom and grandma making these and us kids waiting to sample as soon as they finished frying them. Although making this is quite an elaborate process, for a foodie like me, it is well worth the effort!

Ingredients

60 mins   4-6 ppl

For the Filling
Coconut (Freshly grated): 1 cup
Brown sugar: ¼ cup
Cashews (finely chopped):¼ cup
Small golden Raisins: ¼ cup
Elaichi(Cardamom): 2 to 3 cloves
Dalchini(Cinnamon) powdered: 1 stick (About 1 tsp)
Oil for frying (Vegetable or sunflower oil)

For the Dough
Sooji (Cream of wheat): 2 cups
Sugar: 1 cup
Salt: 1/4th tsp
Water: 3 ½ cups

Method

1. Heat the coconut and brown sugar together, till the water evaporates and the mixture becomes dry.Remove from fire.

2. Add the cashews and raisins while the mixture is still hot. Then add cardamom and cinnamon powder. Your filling is now ready.

3. Next, to make the dough, boil 3 ½ cups of water. Add sugar and stir till it dissolves

4. Add the cream of wheat and then salt. Stir continuously till the water evaporates and it becomes dough like. (This is easier said than done. Make sure you stir constantly. The dough should be firm and not too runny)

5. Remove from fire. Put some oil or butter on your palms and knead the dough for about 5 minutes while it is still warm.

6. Tear off golf ball sized dough.Make into a ball

7. Flatten and knead into the shape of a bowl.

8. Add a teaspoon of filling in it and seal completely to form a ball filled with the dough. (See picture)

9. Repeat till you have used up all the dough (About 15 to 20sooji balls)

10. In a wok, heat 2 cups of oil. Once the oil is sufficiently hot, carefully, lower the stuffed sooji ball into the hot oil and fry till it is golden brown.

11. Blot on a paper to remove excess oil and serve hot.

Note:
This dish stays fresh in the refrigerator for up to 4 days

MANGO MOUSSE PIE
A light fruity mousse

By now you have probably guessed that mango is one of my favourite fruits. In earlier recipes, I have written all about how it brings back childhood memories and how it is more than just a fruit to me. Due to its extremely sweet taste and fleshy, robust texture, the humble mango is quite versatile and can be used for many sweet and savoury dishes.

When we moved to the US, I got to sample a lot of pies; apple pie, peach pie, blueberry, strawberry and even pecan pie. To be honest I really didn't care for any of them except for maybe apple pie; served warm, straight from the oven, with vanilla ice-cream. I experimented with mango and landed up with a fool proof mango pie. Unlike most pies, this is with a mousse base and is typically served cold. It makes for a great summer dessert! Instead of baking, the pie is set in the fridge. Quick, easy and no bake. You are welcome!

Ingredients

chilling time		
4 hrs	10 mins	8-12 ppl

Mango pulp: 2 Cups
Condensed milk: 1cup
Pre made Pie Crust: 1 (In India this would be available in some of the gourmet food stores)
Gelatine: 1 sleeve or 1 tsp
Milk: ¼ Cup

Method

1. Whisk mango pulp, milk and condensed milk in an electric mixer till light and frothy, about 2-3 minutes.

2. Make gelatine as per pack instructions. Add to the mango mixture and whisk again for about 2 minutes.

3. Pour into the pie crust and set in the refrigerator (NOT Freezer) for 4 hours.

4. Decorate with cherries or mint leaves and serve.

Note:
You can use store bought mango pulp if fresh mangoes are not at hand. The gelatine needs to be made and whisked very well otherwise the mixture will have lumps. You can skip the pie crust to set the mousse in decorative glasses for a lower calorie dessert.